recovering origins

A Unique Healing Program for Adult Children of Divorce

MARGARET HARPER McCARTHY

UNDER THE AUSPICES OF THE PONTIFICAL JOHN PAUL II
INSTITUTE FOR STUDIES ON MARRIAGE & FAMILY
AT THE CATHOLIC UNIVERSITY OF AMERICA

Foreword by Carl A. Anderson

CATHOLIC EDUCATION PRESS
WASHINGTON, D.C.

Catholic Education Press
The Catholic University of America
Washington, D.C. 20064

The paper used in this publication meets the minimum requirements
of American National Standards for Information Science—
Permanence of Paper for Printed Library Materials, ANSI Z39.48-1984.

Cataloging-in-Publication data available from the Library of Congress.

ISBN: 978-1-9498-2212-0
eISBN: 978-1-9498-2213-7

Book design by Burt&Burt
Text set in ITC Galliard and Meta Pro

Printed in Canada

RECOVERING ORIGINS

Finally! A resource for the emotional and spiritual healing of the adult children of divorce that does not patronize, shame, or gaslight them for having the feelings and wounds that naturally result from the destruction of their families. Meditating through the Our Father and Scripture, the participants work from their interior life to bind up those wounds, while also receiving practical tools for moving forward toward wholeness—and holiness. There are very few resources for the adult children of divorce that I find worthy of recommendation, and this is one of them.

—Leila Miller
Author of *Primal Loss: The Now-Adult Children of Divorce Speak*

Recovering Origins: A Unique Healing Program for Adult Children of Divorce is a very much needed and truly innovative contribution with its integrated, emotional, prayerful and retreat-based model. I am sure it will benefit many. Perhaps those who benefit from this program may even come to see that their parents' divorce was a disguised blessing because in overcoming it they grew in strength, resilience, and holiness.

—Paul C. Vitz, Ph.D
Professor, Divine Mercy University
Author of *Faith of the Fatherless: The Psychology of Atheism*

This most unique program is a blessing not just to the adult children of divorce but to the Church and to society. *Recovering Origins* offers a fresh start on a solid foundation to those most affected by the divorce of their parents. What is most encouraging is that individuals can draw from their wounds and utilize them as catalysts to heal and become stronger. To offer hope and truth is the best remedy to stop the cycle of divorce. Sadly, when we work with young adults contemplating marriage, they often divulge the fact that they fear entering into a lifelong commitment because they do not want to end up like their parents. Giving them a vision of God's plan and walking them through the healing of their wounds and hearts are such gifts. To turn them toward Our Father, Who Art in Heaven is giving them a solid foundation to build upon and offering them freedom to live an abundant life full of love.

—Julie Alexander
Co-founder, with her husband Greg, of the Alexander House Apostolate and co-author of *Marriage 911: How God Saved Our Marriage and Can Save Yours Too*

"Children of divorce have an ontological wound that evokes metaphysical longings. *Recovering Origins* helps them to find the healing and rest they long for."

—Tory Baucum
Director of the Benedictine Center for Family Life, Benedictine College and Archdiocese of Kansas City

Acknowledgments

Recovering Origins came about as a response to a movement among adult children of divorced parents. After decades of euphemistic talk about the "good divorce," some of them began to speak more forthrightly about the institution that had so marked them, however amical it may have been. The books by Stephanie Staal (*The Love They Lost,* 2000), Elizabeth Marquardt (*Between Two Worlds,* 2005), and Andrew Root (*The Children of Divorce,* 2010) and, more recently, Leila Miller (*Primal Loss,* 2017) are examples of a whole new genre of straight talk about the formerly untouchable *sine qua non* of modern life and its modern (consenting) adults.

The new genre was liberating for many adults who had hitherto not been able—or allowed—to identify the deep-seated disquiet they felt on account of their parents' divorce. The new genre was also radical. It went to the heart of that disquiet. Children are born of the communion of their parents. And they are the literal embodiment of it. When that communion voluntarily dismantles itself, therefore, the effect will not be negligible, nor should it be. Indeed, the new authors described their parents' divorce as a "primal loss," which "pulled them apart," like a "split atom," between what were now "two worlds." Recognizing this, and saying it, these witnesses began to unsettle long-standing doctrines about what it means to be who we are and what it means to love. If we are not quite ourselves when the community that put us into being has wished itself away, then maybe we are not the self-made individuals we all think we are. And if our very being calls for the "forever" of our parents' union, then maybe love isn't after all the temporary feeling and renegotiable arrangement we think it is.

It was thanks precisely to the radical judgment of the new straight talk about divorce, that we saw, paradoxically, a possibility for a fruitful way forward. By going to the depths of things—the loss of and desire for the community at the origin of one's life—we could be opened up to the Community which stands at the root of it all, our *deepest* Origin. "Deep calls to deep," as the psalmist says (Psalm 42:7).

It was Carl Anderson, Supreme Knight of the Knights of Columbus, who first suggested that we, at the John Paul II Institute, write a pastoral resource for adult children of divorce. In response to this invitation, I went with David L. Schindler, then Dean of the Institute, to see now-Bishop William Byrne, then pastor of St. Peter's on Capitol Hill and former chaplain of the Catholic Student Center at the University of Maryland. A man of great pastoral sensibility and incisive judgment, Fr. Bill was the one who suggested a pastoral resource based on the Lord's Prayer. With him, we held several sessions with a group of young adults; some of them were our own students and others were known to Fr. Bill.

Confident that children of divorce had a deep need for what the Christian faith has to offer, especially the prayer Jesus taught his disciples, we brought together a group of advisors for a weekend at the John Paul II Institute. Together we studied the individual petitions of the Our Father and discussed how they might bear on the experience of divorce. We discussed every aspect of the eight sessions—following roughly the eight petitions—from the prayer, to the reflection, to the suggested counsel at the end of each session ("Learning to See"), to the scriptural texts, testimonials, and beautiful images that could be used throughout. Present with me were Andrew Walther, Sister Maximilia Um, Lisa Lickona, Andrew Sodergren, Fr. Vincent de Rosa, Lesley Rice, Dr. Susan Timoney, Nick Bagileo and Regina Koshute. Each of them had a hand in what is now before you.

When the first draft was finished, we began to pilot the program with groups and individuals. Many participants provided generous feedback. Some confirmed much of the existing text, while others called for changes and amplification. We set to work again, revising the text. For that revision I am especially grateful to Sister Mary Madeleine Todd, Lacy Prebula, Regina Koshute, and Dan Meola. Having participated in the pilot programs themselves, each of them was able to offer valuable insights, suggestions for improvements, and many of the actual revisions. I am especially grateful to Dan Meola for his help on the issues of anger, false securities, and boundaries and, more generally, for spearheading much of this work.

After the second draft was complete, a group of our students began to offer *Recovering Origins* retreats. This was initiated by Dan Meola with the help of Alexander Wolfe, Fr. Jim McCormack, Michael Corsini, Sara Hart, and others. Given their success, requests for retreats began to come in from all over the country. The need for what we had to offer was becoming clear. As a result, we decided to make *Recovering Origins* available to everyone to use however they see fit, whether in the context of an organized retreat, a less formal group discussion, or individually. For the final effort of preparing *Recovering Origins* for its published form, I am especially grateful to Dr. Andrew Sodergren and Sr. Maximilia Um, among others, for their help with some of the more delicate sections (on affirmation, forgiveness, and marriages declared null). Finally, I am grateful to Kelley McNutt for copyediting everything with her usual masterful precision.

For more information about *Recovering Origins,* you can contact the John Paul II Institute for Studies on Marriage and the Family at: information@johnpaulii.edu.

Foreword

Carl A. Anderson
Supreme Knight, Knights of Columbus

During the past four decades, an extensive social science body of literature has examined the devasting effects of divorce upon children's psychological health. It is now beyond question that divorce can leave long-lasting emotional trauma affecting the ability of adult children of divorce to create and sustain healthy relationships. Children of divorce have more negative attitudes toward marriage; are less optimistic about the possibility of obtaining healthy, long-lasting marriages; have lower levels of relationship confidence and commitment; and have higher expectations of divorce later in life. It is not uncommon for children of divorce to express a conviction that relationships do not last, a fear of being hurt and rejected, and a distrust of others. Not surprisingly, children of divorce exhibit different behaviors regarding dating, courtship, and romance. They tend toward earlier dating and more sexual partners; decreased commitments to romantic relationships; and higher incidents of failed romances, pregnancy outside of marriage, and abortion. The legacy of divorce affects children's capacity to love and to be loved not only during adolescence but well into adulthood.

According to Georgetown's Center for Applied Research in the Apostolate, 28 percent of Catholics in America—as compared to nearly 40 percent of Protestants and more than 40 percent of those who profess no religion—have been divorced. Nearly 9 percent of Catholics describe their current marital status as divorced.[1] According to the Pew Research Center another 9 percent of Catholic adults who have been divorced are now civilly remarried. Yet these statistics, sufficiently disturbing in themselves, become exceedingly so when considered within the context of the dramatic decline in the marriage rate itself. In the United States the marriage rate has fallen from 75 percent of adults in 1970 to approximately 52 percent in the last decade. Perhaps even more disturbing is that while a quarter of the U.S. population is Catholic, less than 8 percent of marriages were held in a Catholic church in 2011.[2] Whatever their imprecision and ambiguity, such statistics not only establish a trajectory toward long-term social pathologies; they also point to a massive pastoral challenge.

Studies of Catholic disaffiliation find a significant reason given by lapsed Catholics as to why they leave is that when faced with a personal or spiritual crisis, there was no help to be found in their parish community.[3] While many dioceses are already beginning to meet the pastoral challenge of divorce with marriage support ministries and outreach to divorced Catholics, very little exists to assist and care for children of divorce—especially for adult children of divorce. There are few pastoral situations more in need of Pope Francis's vision of the Church as "field hospital" or of the Church that "accompanies" those who suffer than that of families—and especially children—who have been affected by divorce.

Those who find their capacity to love so dramatically impaired, who have no confidence in lasting relationships, and who have an abiding fear of being hurt have a deep need for pastoral accompaniment.

1 http://nineteensixty-four.blogspot.com/2013/09/divorce-still-less-likely-among.html.

2 Emily Macke, "A Fresh Look at Divorce Statistics: Signs of Hope and Concern." https://www.foryourmarriage.org/blogs/a-fresh-look-at-divorce-statistics-signs-of-hope-and-concern.

3 Stephen Bullivant, *Mass Exodus: Catholic Disaffiliation in Britain and America Since Vatican II* (Oxford: Oxford University Press, 2019), 62.

This is all the more the case since secular culture readily confirms their perceptions and encourages acquiescence to them especially in regard to the permanence and exclusivity of marriage. In addition, accelerating developments in biotechnology, artificial intelligence, and gender theory suggest that we have crossed the threshold of changing perceptions not just about sexual morality and social order, but about what constitutes human nature itself.

So what is an adequate response by those who believe the human person is created in the image and likeness of God: created out of love, for love, and called to a life of communion? How is it possible in these circumstances to convey to wounded individuals this communal dimension of the *Imago Dei*, that is, of a person called to be a gift of one person for another "indicative of a unity of persons that is created by mutual love"?[4]

In 2008, the Knights of Columbus and the Pontifical John Paul II Institute for Studies on Marriage and Family convened an International Congress in Rome titled, *Oil on the Wounds: A Contemporary Examination of the Effects of Divorce and Abortion on Children and Their Families*. The Congress brought together some of the world's leading experts on the impact of divorce upon children including Joan Kelly and Elizabeth Marquardt.[5] The reference to the Good Samaritan in the title of the Congress was an intentional reference not only to the gospel parable, but to the address of Pope St. Paul VI at the conclusion of the Second Vatican Council. There he described charity as the "principal religious feature" of the council and the "old story of the Samaritan" as the model of its spirituality. The Church did not present condemnations, but was "permeated" by a "feeling of boundless sympathy" for the human needs which it encounters."[6]

4 Jaroslaw Kupczak, *Gift and Communion: John Paul II's Theology of the Body* (Washington, D.C.: The Catholic University of America Press, 2014), 149.

5 The proceedings of the Congress were published in English, Spanish and French. Livio Melina and Carl A. Anderson, *Oil on the Wounds: A Contemporary Examination of the Effects of Divorce and Abortion on Children and their Families* (Garden City Park, N.Y.: Square One Publishers, 2011); *Aceite en las Heridas: Análisis y Respuestas a los Dramas del Aborto y del Divorcio* (Madrid: Ediciones Palabra, 2010); and *De l'Huile surles Blessures: Une réponse aux plaies du Divorce et de l'Avortement* (Paris: Editions Parole et Silence, 2009).

6 Pope Paul VI, *Address During the Last General Meeting of the Second Vatican Council*, December 7, 1965.

In his address to the International Congress, Pope Benedict XVI picked up this theme saying, "Only by assuming an attitude of merciful love is it possible to approach to bring help." And he continued: "The Church's first duty is to approach these people with love and consideration, with caring and motherly attention, to proclaim the merciful closeness of God in Jesus Christ. . . . [I]t is he who is the true Good Samaritan, who has made himself close to us, who pours oil and wine on our wounds and takes us into the inn, the Church, where he has us treated, entrusting us to her ministers and personally paying in advance for our recovery."[7]

How appropriate then, that *Recovering Origins* developed by the Pontifical John Paul II Institute in Washington, D.C., takes up the pastoral challenge confronting the adult children of divorce by inviting them to draw close to the loving communion of God the Son with God the Father as revealed in the words of the Lord's Prayer. This is more appropriate still when one realizes that a consequence of divorce is that children find it more difficult to pray and, as a result, suffer a diminished spiritual life and participation in life of the Church.[8] "Lord, teach us to pray," is at once a more complex and more urgent task for children of divorce. As such, it is the most appropriate place to begin. What is needed is a spiritual recovery which, in turn, requires an adequate grounding in an authentic theological anthropology. Thus, from a pastoral perspective we begin with a question that reflects both the anthropological and the spiritual: What does it mean to pray with the words, "*Our Father*"?

Recovering Origins is a unique pastoral initiative that finds in the Lord's Prayer a path that can lead to both discovery and healing for children of divorce. Its eight sessions, each beginning with prayer based in the Psalms, offers participants meditations, reflections, and questions to lead them to see the possibility that human love—even wounded love—can be caught up in Divine love. In other words, *Recovering Origins* offers children of divorce a way in which to recover

7 Pope Benedict XVI, *Address to International Congress: Oil on the Wounds*, April 5, 2008.

8 Patrick F. Fagan and Aaron Churchill, *The Effects of Divorce on Children* (Washington, D.C.: Marriage and Religion Research Institute, 2012), https://marri.us.

a new and profound perception of their ultimate origin in the love of God Himself.

The first session, entitled "Where We Stand," invites participants to face with honesty (at last!) the impact of their parents' divorce on their lives. At the same time, it invites them to look beyond their own experience of a broken love to the ultimate love at the origin of their being: the love of God the Father, who created them, and regenerates them anew in Jesus Christ, through his Church. Each of the sessions that follow focuses on a petition of the Lord's Prayer beginning with "Our Father who art in heaven" in Session II, and ending in Session VII with "Lead us not into temptation, but deliver us from evil." This concluding reflection on the prayer Christ taught us is accompanied by a consideration of the Sacrament of Reconciliation with specific examinations for children of divorce. The emphasis on the fundamental importance of mercy is also seen in Session VI which explores "Forgive us our trespasses" with a consideration of the Chaplet of Divine Mercy. The program concludes in Session VIII with the theme "Who Am I? Plumbing the Depths and Beginning Again." This pastoral initiative recognizes that "as children of divorce, we live with a wound that is sometimes unbearable." But in this suffering, there is a place to find the Lord, for he entered our suffering and transformed it. The program concludes with the introduction of the *Angelus* as a prayer that helps us to see that the Father's love can make all things new and redeem even the most broken heart.

In the context of one of the great pastoral challenges confronting Christians today, *Recovering Origins* offers a profound response founded upon both an honest assessment of the sociological and psychological realities of divorce and the answer offered in the theological and spiritual richness of the One who is indeed rich in mercy. Individuals can work through the eight sessions either together (in a retreat setting) or alone. Each approach has been found beneficial. *Recovering Origins* should not only be on the bookshelves of every rectory and chancery, but also available throughout every diocese as an ongoing program, and in seminaries as a formative pastoral guide in the evangelization of marriage and family life.

Introduction

The pastoral initiative *Recovering Origins* is offered to adult children of divorced parents who, now at a certain distance from the practical difficulties that burden younger children, wrestle with the core problem at the heart of those difficulties. They have lost the community that brought them into the world and, as a result, have suffered a primal loss. Taking that loss seriously, *Recovering Origins* aims to help adult children of divorce let their wounds become a place of contact with God's love so that they can come to know what most deeply defines them, that their lives are good, and that an irrevocable and fruitful love is possible. It invites participants to move through the broken image of love that they see in their parents to the Love that stands at the origin of their being.

Recovering Origins begins with an invitation to look freely and honestly at the experience of divorce, beyond all the "happy talk" about "the good divorce." Participants are then invited to follow the path of the Lord's Prayer, to recover what is at once challenging and precious to those whose very identities are on uncertain ground: the memory of God the Father, that loving Origin which is deeper than any human reflection of it—broken or not. In this way, the program offers a path to healing in the deepest sense, even if some effects of divorce remain.

The path of the Lord's Prayer proposed by *Recovering Origins* offers an occasion to encounter the faith more deeply, especially where it bears on fundamental questions faced by children of divorce in a particularly dramatic way: questions about identity, love, and destiny. In this way, then, *Recovering Origins* addresses adult children of divorce not just as individuals in need of pastoral care, but as potential witnesses to something they can often see more clearly: the longing in every heart to know the One on whom their lives ultimately depend.

GENERAL INSTRUCTIONS AND OVERVIEW OF EACH SESSION

There are eight sessions in the *Recovering Origins* program. These sessions can be discussed in a group or read on one's own. Ideally, participants would go through these sessions in the company of others and under the guidance of a priest or some other guide. A group might consist of other adult children of divorce or a couple preparing for marriage or in need of marriage counseling. It might be just an individual with a counselor. Guides should be persons with some direct experience of divorce, either by being adult children of divorce themselves, or by having counseled them. Most importantly guides should be capable of giving witness to the experience and reasonableness of the faith, especially as it bears on the deep wounds of divorce. They should be able to offer a witness to Christ's healing. (The literature in the "General Resources" section at the end may be of some help to potential guides.)

The program can be conducted anywhere interested parties wish to gather—home, parish, workplace, etc.—provided it is a place free from distraction where one can be reflective and attentive to oneself and to others.

A group setting is, however, by no means necessary. A participant may already have friends with whom to discuss these matters informally and may already have the experience of a rich ecclesial community, where one can tangibly experience the fundamental goodness of one's life. In that case, he or she may benefit by simply reading these materials alone. It is necessary, however, to go through the sessions in a reflective manner. To this end, participants might consider keeping a journal.

Each of the sessions begins with prayer based on the Psalms. It can be prayed antiphonally when there is a group. Following the prayer is a reflection on a petition of the Our Father. At points, personal testimonies are provided by adult children of divorce who chronicle their own experience. In a group, the reflection can be read together or presented by the guide or by a participant—whichever is best. The group can, naturally, pause at any point to discuss a section or two with the help of the questions offered (or any others that might arise spontaneously). At the end of each session there is a proposed daily prayer taken from the rich treasury of Catholic tradition. This section is called "Learning to See" because it is offered as way to help us see the Love that ultimately defines us.

Specific themes for each session are as follows:

- **Session I: Where We Stand** takes stock of where children of divorce stand and names the deepest wound of divorce.

- **Session II: "Our Father Who Art in Heaven"** helps children of divorce discover their deepest identity as sons and daughters of God the Father; explores how divorce affects this identity, especially through the lack of affirmation; and helps children of divorce recover this identity by developing a deeper awareness of their relationship with God, grounded in their Baptism.

- **Session III: "Hallowed Be Thy Name"** helps children of divorce discover who God is; teaches how divorce affects their understanding of God; and helps them recover an adequate image of God.

- **Session IV: "Thy Kingdom Come, Thy Will Be Done on Earth as It Is in Heaven"** teaches God's plan for marriage and family; it helps children of divorce understand how the experience of their parents' divorce affects their pursuit of love, and how the Church's teachings and life offer a truer path forward.

- **Session V: "Give Us This Day Our Daily Bread"** shows children of divorce how to address anger and face their anxiety about the future by entrusting it to God, who supplies their deepest needs—*daily*—especially in the Sacrament of the Eucharist.

- **Session VI: "Forgive Us Our Trespasses, as We Forgive Those Who Trespass Against Us"** discusses what Christian forgiveness is, especially the forgiveness of one's parents.

- **Session VII: "Lead Us Not into Temptation, But Deliver Us from Evil"** addresses sinful tendencies common in children of divorce, especially the tendency to doubt God's goodness and to place security in the wrong things; it encourages children of divorce to seek mercy and forgiveness in God through the Sacrament of Reconciliation.

- **Session VIII: Who Am I? Plumbing the Depths and Beginning Again** helps children of divorce discover how their own experience can actually be a resource for the world, because their need to know the original Love on whom their lives ultimately depend is also the world's need; it introduces participants to the accompaniment of Mary and all the saints, those in heaven and those on earth.

WHAT PARTICIPANTS HAVE SAID

"I think it is profoundly beautiful that each passage was led by sections of the Our Father. This has actually helped me see the Our Father in a different more personal light! Like a conversation with God!"

"It put into words all the things I've experienced and couldn't quite explain in a clear and accurate manner."

"The reflection presents ideas I had never come across before! The description of normal childhood and security versus loss of play! It described my situation."

"The 'Learning to See' is wonderful. To learn to look habitually on the Father's Love, to practice seeing. So totally new!"

"I very much like the proposition (and practice!) of praying the *Angelus* to remember my true identity as a son of God in Christ and the promise of Jesus Christ to be born in me so that I may love like him."

"I think the program is absolutely beautiful. I just recently got engaged over Christmas and the first few reflections in particular struck me. Even after years of being immersed in the Church's teachings on love, identity, and of course marriage and family, the struggle to accept, believe, and trust in my deeper identity in God the Father remains. Particularly as my fiancée and I begin our marriage preparation, the issues from my parents' divorce, which was over a decade ago, are at the forefront of my mind. The program articulates in a very easy to understand way the emotions, fears, and struggles of the adult child of divorce."

recovering origins

SESSION I

Where We Stand

My tears have been my food day and night.
Psalm 42:3

PRAYER

Opening

L: Lord, open my lips.

R: And my mouth will proclaim your praise.

Psalm 42

L: In Psalm 42, the psalmist sings a lament that also is a prayer of trust in God's providence. His heart is heavy because he is far away from his homeland and from the Temple, the heart of Jewish life. . . .

L: As a deer longs for flowing streams, so longs my soul for you, O God. My soul thirsts for God, for the living God. When shall I come and behold the face of God?

R: Hope in God, for I shall again praise him, my help and my God.

L: My tears have been my food day and night, while men say to me continually,

L: "Where is your God?" These things I remember, as I pour out my soul: how I went with the throng, and led them in procession to the house of God, with glad shouts and songs of thanksgiving, a multitude keeping festival.

R: Hope in God, for I shall again praise him, my help and my God.

L: Why are you cast down, O my soul, and why are you disquieted within me? Hope in God; for I shall again praise him, my savior and my God.

R: Hope in God, for I shall again praise him, my help and my God.

L: My soul is cast down within me, therefore I remember you from the land of Jordan and of Hermon from Mount Mizar. Deep calls to deep at the thunder of your cataracts;
all your waves and your billows have gone over me.

R: Hope in God, for I shall again praise him, my help and my God.

L: By day the LORD commands his steadfast love; and at night his song is with me, a prayer to the God of my life. I say to God, my rock: "Why have you forgotten me? Why do I go mourning because of the oppression of the enemy?"

R: Hope in God, for I shall again praise him, my help and my God.

L: As with a deadly wound in my body, my adversaries taunt me, while they say to me continually, "Where is your God?" Why are you cast down, O my soul, and why are you disquieted within me? Hope in God; for I shall again praise him, my help and my God.

R: Hope in God, for I shall again praise him, my help and my God.

Reading

Reader:
A Reading from the Gospel according to Matthew (7:7–11)

Ask, and it will be given you; seek, and you will find; knock, and it will be opened to you. For everyone who asks receives, and he who seeks finds, and to him who knocks it will be opened. Or what man of you, if his son asks him for bread, will give him a stone? Or if he asks for a fish, will give him a serpent? If you then, who are evil, know how to give good gifts to your children, how much more will your Father who is in heaven give good things to those who ask him!

(Prayer in Silence)

Closing Prayer

L: Confident that God, our Father, hears all our prayers, we pray the prayer that Jesus taught us.

All: Our Father who art in heaven. . . .

L: Glory be to the Father and to the Son and to the Holy Spirit.

R: As it was in the beginning, is now and ever shall be, world without end. Amen.

REFLECTION

In this session, we are taking stock of where we stand as children of divorce. We are looking at our experience square in the face. Why? Because we sense that what marks us so deeply cannot be swept under the rug. But most of all, because we have reasons to be confident that we can pass through the experience of divorce to reach a more original experience lodged in the depths of our hearts, a more original and definitive love—the Love that made us.

Naturally, people have different readings of their lives lived in the wake of divorce. Some of us remain devastated by it in more obvious ways. Others of us are not so visibly affected by the experience and have "gotten over it." It may not even be so clear that there is a problem.

Indeed, some of us have become convinced of what many have told us: that things *had* to go the way they did, that it was "all for the better."

So when we stop to consider the impact of our parents' divorce on our lives, we may at first tell ourselves that it was insignificant. From the time we were children, we learned to successfully negotiate the complex situations in our families. We learned to manage the transitions, the breakups, the remarriages, perhaps even the second divorces. Managing the transitions has even made some of us "stronger," "more resilient." By all measurable standards many of us are "successful." We got good grades, went to college, got jobs, even started families of our own.

Do I see myself reflected in these descriptions or would I describe my experience differently?

Signs of a Wound

As we entered adulthood, however, we most likely began to feel that even though our lives appeared successful on the outside, there was a deep and open wound on the inside. We realized that the divorce remained a decisive moment in our lives, so much so that we divided our own personal histories into "before the divorce" and "after the divorce."

One of the ways in which the wound inside of us shows itself is in the way we think about and approach love—whether in our families, friendships, or marriages. Given our experience of the rift in our parents' marriage, we often harbor an underlying cynicism about the goodness of things, and above all, the goodness of love and of its promise to be "forever." One child of divorce said:

> In my most desperate moments, I think to myself, "If my parents can get divorced, then any good thing can disappear."
>
> —Quoted in Judith Wallerstein
> *The Unexpected Legacy of Divorce*, xxii

As a result of this cynicism about love, we struggle with anxiety in our friendships and marriages. Another child of divorce said:

Pablo Picasso, *The Tragedy* (1903), The National Gallery of Art, Washington, DC ►

1903
Picasso

> About marriage . . . part of me is always waiting for disaster to strike. . . . I'm always waiting for the other shoe to drop.
>
> —Quoted in Judith Wallerstein
> *The Unexpected Legacy of Divorce*, xxii

This anxiety, then, sabotages our ability to move forward, especially when it comes to forming long lasting friendships. If we do manage to "tie the knot," we often find ourselves drained of the energy needed to persevere. We find that we have few spiritual and psychological resources for doing our part to keep things going. The underlying cynicism we have about the possibility of an enduring love has taken its toll.

Have I found it difficult
to form or to maintain relationships?

At the Heart of the Wound

No matter how much our parents individually love us, we have lost our parents' love *together.*

> What children grieve is not the loss of love *directed toward them*, but the loss of the mysterious and powerful community of love that existed before them and elected to invite them into the world.
>
> —Andrew Root
> *Children of Divorce*, 81

As the fruit of our parents' unity, we may question our very selves. We may wonder, *Why was I not worth my parents staying together? Is there something wrong with me?* At the heart of things, the failure of our parents' vows hits us at the point of our very origin, and therefore of our identity. Some have described the wound of divorce as existence between two separate worlds.

> As I entered young adulthood I began to sense that growing up with parents in two different worlds, with me traveling between them, had shaped me in profound ways.
>
> —Elizabeth Marquardt
> *Between Two Worlds*, 8–9

The cover of a book written for young children of divorce, Adolph Moser's *Don't Fall Apart on Saturdays! The Children's Divorce-Survival Book*, portrays this tellingly with an illustration of a girl whose limbs are literally being pulled apart. Others have even suggested the experience of annihilation, akin to a nuclear explosion.

> [My parents' divorce] split the atom of my existence straight down the middle, leaving me to cope with a lifetime of emotional fall-out. . . . I who, in their love letters, they had called "our little angel" was now referred to—in correspondence with their lawyers—as "the child." Later on I became "that bloody child" (my mother, at her worse when I didn't agree with the divorce) or that "poor confused child" (my father and stepmother, also not at their best.) I dwell on these epithets only because they epitomized the state of being, the fractured ontology, with which I would have to struggle thereafter.
>
> —Nicky Rowdon
> "Cold War," *Humanum* (Spring 2012)

Reasons to Hesitate

We may hesitate to examine something so painful, something which touches our identity so deeply. We may also fear unsettling our parents, many of whom love us very much. We may fear their rejection, or the rejection of others who minimize our "baggage." Above all, we may be skeptical, thinking that nothing good will come out of this examination. Here is the testimony of one child of divorce who travelled the road we are proposing and is skeptical no more!

I was in sixth grade when my parents separated. I vowed that I would never be like my mother and father in dating relationships. Nonetheless, following the aftermath and despite my best resolutions, I ended up in bad patterns. There was the cynical "take-what-you-can-get" stage, the romantic "she-is-my-savior" stage, and everything in-between. At times, I took on the roles of the people-pleaser, the rescuer, the perfectionist, and the excessive peacemaker. None of these were healthy and several relationships failed. Through various life events, I realized I could not keep running from the pain and doing things on my own. I needed Christ to heal the wounds. Dwelling in his love on a daily basis, he slowly brought healing to the underlying wound of my parents' divorce, helped me to exchange my unhealthy behaviors for virtue, through Saint John Paul II's *Theology of the Body*, and gave me a renewed vision and belief in love and marriage.

Eventually, when I was twenty-six, I took the risk (there is always one!) and entered into the Sacrament of Marriage with my wonderful wife Bethany. We've been happily married now for nine years and have two beautiful children. I still struggle with certain problems, like handling conflict, but I now trust the Lord to help me through it and recognize the great gift of shared mercy to sustain a marriage. Christ is close to us as a couple. He promises that "perfect love drives out fear" (I John 4:18), a promise so important that we engraved this verse onto our wedding bands and recall it often. Indeed, this perfect love of Christ has been healing my heart—and my wife's—through the great gift of marriage open to the sanctifying beauty of grace.

—Daniel Meola, Ph.D.
Co-founder and president of Life-Giving Wounds
Ministry for Adult Children of Divorce or Separation

A More Original Experience

The point of taking stock of our situation is not so that we can wallow in self-pity or point fingers at our parents. On the contrary, we recognize the deep wound inside of us in order to be brought face to

Henri Matisse, *Icarus* (1947), The Metropolitan Museum of Art, New York, NY ▶

face with a deeper, *more original* experience, one that is even more definitive than the wounds that have so marked us. That more original experience is lodged in the "heart," at the "core" of our being, even if many layers of "sediment" (the wounds of sin), have settled on top and hidden it. It is the experience of a truer and more faithful Love, the Love that made us and calls out to us now.

However much we have been begotten by our parents, they are not the ultimate origin and source of our being. God is. Parents *participate* with him, by *procreating*. And however much they are his image, they are not identical to him. We must not stop at the image. Rather, we must look through the image—which is now also broken—and catch a glimpse of the deeper, truer Love at the origin of our being. We must entreat him to show his face. God, in fact, is offering this glimpse right now. In his Son, he loves us with the profound tenderness of a father and a mother. He is moved by our suffering. He sees us in our brokenness, our misery, our struggles, and he desires to give us everything we need.

> Can a woman forget her sucking child, that she should have no compassion on the son of her womb? Even these may forget, yet I will not forget you.
>
> —*Isaiah 49:15*

> If you then, who are evil, know how to give good gifts to your children, how much more will your Father who is in heaven give good things to those who ask him!
>
> —*Matthew 7:11*

We can begin to recover our identity by recovering our Origin.

LEARNING TO SEE: THE "OUR FATHER"

It is a temptation to think that what has happened to us is the definitive word on love. For this reason, it is important to *learn to see* the Love which is behind—and more constant than—our parents' love. To see the deepest truth of things requires education and, above all, practice. It is a question of knowing how to pierce the surface of everyday life in order to find what is *most true*. To that end, we propose a prayer or practice from the rich Catholic tradition to be taken up after each session, every day (or hour) until the next one. We suggest, too, that any fruits from this prayer be documented in a journal so that they can be *remembered* in times of doubt or shared with others.

Here, we begin with the prayer that Jesus taught his disciples, the Our Father. The Our Father is the common thread of this entire program because it is the most simple and beautiful way to go to the heart of the need we have, to *recover our origin*. As the *Catechism of the Catholic Church* says:

> In *Baptism* and *Confirmation* the handing on (*traditio*) of the Lord's Prayer signifies new birth into the divine life. Since Christian prayer is our speaking to God with the very word of God, those who are "born anew" . . . through the "living and abiding word of God" (I Peter 1:23) learn to invoke their Father by the one Word he always hears. They can henceforth do so, for the seal of the Holy Spirit's anointing is indelibly placed on their hearts, ears, lips, indeed their whole filial being. . . . When the Church prays the Lord's Prayer, it is always the people made up of the "new-born" who pray and obtain mercy.
>
> —*CCC*, 2769

After this session, then, pray the Our Father every day.

Our Father who art in heaven,
hallowed be thy name.
Thy kingdom come.
Thy will be done
on earth, as it is in heaven.
Give us this day our daily bread,
and forgive us our trespasses,
as we forgive those who trespass against us,
and lead us not into temptation,
but deliver us from evil.

SESSION II

"Our Father Who Art in Heaven"

For this reason, I bow my knees before the Father,
from whom every family in heaven and on earth is named.
Ephesians 3:14

PRAYER

Opening

L: Lord, open my lips.

R: And my mouth will proclaim your praise.

L: Lord send the fire of your Holy Spirit deep within us, so that we can serve you with devotion and please you with our hearts, minds, and actions. We pray this through Christ our Lord. Amen.

Our Father

L: The following prayer is a meditation on the Our Father that St. Francis of Assisi liked to pray as a way of deepening his understanding and love of the prayer that Jesus taught.

L: O, our most holy Father,

All: Our Creator, Redeemer, Consoler, and Savior

L: Who are in heaven:

All: *In the angels and in the saints,*
enlightening them to love, because you, Lord are light;
Inflaming them to love, because you Lord are love;
Dwelling (in them) and filling them with happiness, because you, Lord, are the Supreme Good, the Eternal Good, from whom comes all good, without whom there is no good.

L: Hallowed be your name:

All: *May our knowledge of you become ever clearer.*
That we may know the breadth of your blessings;
the length of your promises;
the height of your majesty;
the depth of your judgments.

L: Your kingdom come:

All: *So that you may rule in us through your grace and enable us to come to your kingdom*
where there is an unclouded vision of you;
a perfect love of you;
a blessed companionship with you;
an eternal enjoyment of you.

L: Your will be done on earth as it is in heaven

All: *We may love you with our whole heart by always thinking of you;*
with our whole soul by always desiring you;
with our whole mind by directing all our intentions to you and by seeking your glory in everything;
and with our whole strength by spending all our energies and affections of soul and body
in the service of your love and of nothing else.
And may we love our neighbors as ourselves
by drawing them all with our whole strength to your love;
by rejoicing in the good fortunes of others as well as our own;
by sympathizing with the misfortunes of others;
and by giving offense to no one.

L: Give us this day,

All: In memory and understanding of and reverence for the love which our Lord Jesus Christ had for us and of those things which he said and did and suffered for us.

L: Our daily bread:

All: Your own beloved Son, our Lord Jesus Christ.

L: And forgive us our trespasses,

All: Through your ineffable mercy;
through the power of the Passion of your beloved Son;
together with the merits and intercession of the Blessed Virgin Mary
and all your chosen ones.

L: As we forgive those who trespass against us.

All: And whatever we do not forgive perfectly, do you, Lord, enable us to forgive to the full so that we may truly love our enemies,
and fervently intercede for them before you;
returning no one evil for evil
and striving to help everyone in you.

L: And lead us not into temptation:

All: Hidden or obvious, sudden or persistent.

L: But deliver us from evil:

All: Past, present, and to come.

L: Glory be to the Father and to the Son and to the Holy Spirit:

All: As it was in the beginning, is now, and ever shall be, world without end. Amen.

Note: Prayer adapted from Benedict Groeschel, *Stumbling Blocks or Stepping Stones: Spiritual Answers to Psychological Questions* (Mahwah, New Jersey: Paulist Press, 1987), 151–153.

REFLECTION

In the first session, we began to take stock of the situation in which we find ourselves. We began to consider how the experience of our parents' divorce may have affected our sense of identity in relation to our Father in heaven. No matter how successful or adjusted we may feel, the divorce of our parents has left many of us with a nagging sense of brokenness at the deepest level. That brokenness, in turn, has affected how we relate to others—above all, to God. In this session we will begin to examine some of the reasons why that may be.

A marriage brings together a man and a woman from two different families. They come from two "worlds," so to speak. When they enter the new reality of marriage, they become one "world." They then begin to give that world a concrete expression by making a home. When children are born, they are the further embodiment of their parents' "world," for they are the fruit of their mutual love, the giving and receiving of the mother and the father. So it is that each child is meant to discover that he or she is loved and wanted in the "home" of the mutual love of his or her parents. There, parents take delight in the simple fact of the presence of their children. And there, children receive the first and most basic lesson of their entire education: that their value resides fundamentally in their existence itself, apart from any good or useful action they may perform. *It is good that I exist!* It is this experience of affirmation in the one "world" of parental love that opens the child to the capacity to receive love and enables him or her to grow in emotional and spiritual maturity.

One of the concrete ways in which we experience love in our childhood is when we play. In play, we are *allowed to be.* We let our imaginations take flight and do things just for the fun of it—just because—with no worries about how long something takes or what it will accomplish. Standing in the background is the presence and protection of our parents; behind them is the presence of God who loves us *for our own sake.*

Our belonging to our parents is like a thread that connects us to our even deeper belonging to God. When we pray "Our Father who art in heaven," we acknowledge this.

Loss of Childhood

When parents get divorced, the dynamics of the family dramatically change. Suddenly, the common work of pursuing a life together—of making of a home—ends. Now there are two separated people going in two separate directions. The children left in the wake of a divorce must now negotiate between what have become two separate worlds. They must go back and forth—often literally—between two houses, deal with two sets of rules, and even behave like two different people (silencing one side of themselves, then the other).

Bartolomé Murillo, *Holy Family with the Little Bird* (c. 1650), Museo del Prado, Madrid, Spain

> When there are two family worlds, the child is asked to do the impossible. To find his being in two opposed worlds, he is asked to be two people.
>
> —Andrew Root
> *Children of Divorce*, 85

It is as though the ground that the children had previously been standing on has been pulled out from underneath them and they are left suspended in the air between an ever-growing gap. After a divorce, most children have a home in the sense of a place (or places) to live; they often have a great deal of love from each of their parents, taken individually. What they have lost, though, is the home that their parents built together as an expression of their love for each other. They have lost their common life.

Not surprisingly, many of us have difficulty remembering times of play after our parents' divorce. We often became little adults, forced to take up the daunting responsibility of creating a new world in place of the one that our parents had previously provided. While we struggled to adjust to the new reality into which we were thrust, we were often left to fend for ourselves.

> [T]he central, daunting task that was suddenly assigned to us following our parents' divorce was this: we, and we alone, had to try to make sense of our parents' increasingly different ways of living. The most important models for our own budding identities—our mother and our father—no longer had the job of rubbing the rough edges of their own worlds together in an attempt to hand us something reasonably whole.
>
> —Elizabeth Marquardt
> *Between Two Worlds*, 29

In the wake of the divorce, we felt less free just "to be" and to do things "just because." The *togetherness* of our parents that made that freedom possible was now gone. And our childhood disappeared with it.

Pablo Picasso, *Child with a Dove* (1901), National Gallery, London, UK ►

Does this description resonate? Did I grow up too fast? How did the loss of my childhood home affect me? Did I experience the disorientation of living between two worlds?

Precocious "Adulthood" and Its Deeper Implications

As a result of our premature loss of childhood, some of us wonder whether childhood itself makes any sense, whether it makes any sense to be dependent on the affirmation of anyone other than ourselves.

> My resourcefulness and independence were sources of pride. Sometimes this role was a burden to me, but I also accepted it as part of my identity. It didn't occur to me that there was another way of living. I felt I had only myself to rely on. But if I was mature on the outside, inside I was still a child, often lonely, sometimes confused, and sometimes very scared. When I was home alone or taking care of my brother, I imagined strangers peeping through our windows or looking through the skylight of my attic bedroom.
>
> Unfortunately, my parents did not have room for feelings such as these. My mother was too overwhelmed, and my father lived too far away to even know about them.
>
> —Elizabeth Marquardt
> *Between Two Worlds*, 34

We have worked hard to be grown-up, unaffected by others and independent of them. And since our parents' love is supposed to teach us about the nature of God's love, we have been tempted to be independent of him as well.

This opens up yet another problem. If we cannot be children in the deepest sense—trusting and waiting upon the affirmation of God—will it be possible for us to be adults in the truest sense? Will we be capable of binding ourselves irrevocably to another for the sake of a fruitful life? Fearful that we cannot entrust ourselves to anyone, many of us settle for temporary relationships, ones that can easily be dissolved. And when the time comes to get married, many of us experience a paralyzing anxiety about lifelong commitment. Many of us don't want to become mothers or fathers. We wonder: *Can we create a home? Can we create a place of affirmation and welcome for children?* It is easy to feel that we are left without resources, exposed and alone.

Did I experience a loss of childhood? Does it affect my ability to trust God? How does that affect me as an adult, in my understanding of who I am, and in my capacity to give myself to another and to others?

Our Need for Affirmation

Our insecurity can spring in part from an intuition that we are unable to give ourselves because we don't yet fully possess ourselves. According to psychiatrist Dr. Conrad Baars, self-possession comes to us as a gift when another "affirms our being," that is, when another takes an unfeigned and ungrasping delight in the fact that we exist. Baars writes:

> In order to become you, you must first *receive* the gift of yourself. In order to receive this gift, there has to be another who *gives*, who gives without taking, without demanding anything, who gives you what is not his own, but yours, your own goodness. The other can do this only when he is already happy with himself, and thus open to the goodness of all else.
>
> —Conrad Baars
> *Born Only Once: The Miracle of Affirmation*, 19–20

When I see the telltale signs in the countenance and manner of another person that he or she is not eyeing me as a mere tool to be used for his or her own purposes, but rather is authentically moved with delight at who I am, he or she becomes a mirror to me, revealing the foundational truth about myself that it is good that I exist. This affirmation of my being enables me to begin to see myself through the Father's eyes. I slowly start to recognize that my presence on this earth is a joy-producing good and a gift to the world. Secured in this experiential knowledge of my own innate dignity, I am free to recognize and respond with delight at the beauty of the world around me and grow in the capacity to bestow on others the same affirmation that I have first received. I am able to *give myself* as a gift because I have *first received myself* as gift.

While no one can mediate this affirming truth of the Father's delight in us perfectly, the sanctuary of our parents' emotionally mature love for us is the normal place where our education in affirmation begins. But what happens if our parents' own woundedness made them unable to adequately offer us this gift, or our experience of it in the formative years of childhood was cut prematurely short through the stress of divorce? Baars warns that when children are deprived of the foundational experience of affirmation, they can come to believe that they are valuable only for what they can provide others and will often spend their lives trying to earn love through actions intended to force others to love them.

Many unaffirmed adults focus all their energy desperately trying to please others, while others turn to aggressive behavior to assert their self-worth. Such attempts at "self-affirmation" end up being self-defeating, for even when they are met with approval, children of divorce will merely conclude that their value comes solely from their usefulness. This compels them to work even harder to try to fill the unrelenting void in their hearts. Whether it takes the form of striving after material goods, asserting power, seeking the approval of others, sexual promiscuity, the pursuit of pleasure, aggressive or even homicidal activity, Baars argues that all such attempts to validate ourselves in the eyes of others are doomed to fail. We end up pushing them away and strengthening the cycle of rejection, withdrawal, and despair in ways that leave no room for healing through authentic affirmation.

According to Baars, our healing comes when we have the courage to let go of our self-sabotaging attempts to manipulate love and allow our true selves to be seen through the vulnerability of authenticity. We must stop living our lives as a performance for others and allow ourselves to be who we are, regardless of what people think of us. Only in being truly ourselves, as a gift from God, will others be able to see who we really are and bless us with the gift of affirmation.

Naturally not everyone is capable of affirmation. The capacity to affirm requires persons who are emotionally mature and happy in themselves. Not all relationships, therefore, are places where we can be seen for who we really are. Thus, on our road to healing we must sometimes step away from unhealthy or abusive relationships and ask the Father to send new people into our lives, people who can affirm us truly by proclaiming in word and deed: "It is good that you exist."

Ultimately what we seek is someone who can manifest *God's* affirmation of our being, the affirmation at the origin of our existence. That is what the first disciples encountered in encountering the Son of God in the flesh. Here is a description of what the "apostle to the apostles" experienced when she was met by the affirming gaze of Christ.

> Mary Magdalene is there on the sidewalk, curious—like all women, but she above all—watching the crowd following that man Jesus who calls himself the Messiah. (They would kill him a few months later). And Jesus, passing by for an instant, without even stopping, looks at her. From that moment, she will no longer look at herself, she will no longer see herself, and she will no longer see men, the crowd, her house, Jerusalem, the world, the rain and the sun . . . she will no longer be able to look at these things other than through the gaze of his eyes. When she looked at herself in the mirror, her countenance was dominated, determined by those eyes. Those eyes were in there. Her face was shaped by them. . . . Throughout her life—in the details and in the whole—Mary Magdalene was looked at inside by that gaze without a single word. Her entire life—in the details and in the whole—she could not see, not feel, nor live except inside that gaze.
>
> —Servant of God Luigi Giussani
> *Dal temperamento un metodo*
> (A Method of Temperament), 5–6 [my translation]

Because the Church makes Christ a contemporary of every man, the experience of Christ's gaze can be ours today—and just as tangible as it was for the first disciples.

Does Conrad Baars's description of the importance of affirmation resonate with my experience? Do I find myself striving to affirm myself in the unhealthy ways described above? Do I experience true affirmation anywhere? Does anyone in my life manifest the affirming gaze of Christ?

A New Childhood

Naming the wounds we carry as a result of our parents' divorce can be both validating and frightening. We may find ourselves grieving anew over the premature loss of our childhood and worrying that our broken past will rob us of a promising future. Dare we hope that the grief of our youth can be conquered and transformed? Pope St. John Paul II addressed just this concern during the 2002 World Youth Day when he boldly testified:

> Although I have lived through much darkness, under harsh totalitarian regimes, I have seen enough evidence to be unshakably convinced that no difficulty, no fear is so great that it can completely suffocate *the hope that springs eternal in the hearts of the young*. . . . Do not let that hope die! Stake your lives on it! *We are not the sum total of our weaknesses and failures;* we are the sum of the Father's love for us and our real capacity to become the image of his Son.
>
> —St. John Paul II
> *World Youth Day*, Toronto, 2002

We are the sum of the Father's love for us! It is this love that ultimately stands at the origin of our being. This love created us, inviting us into being, and continues to hold us in being. It is the root of everything. The fate of our parents' union is powerless to contradict or rob us of this fact.

> [T]he apostle Philip confusedly intuited when, just an hour before Christ was arrested, he asked him, "Continue to speak to us of the Father; just for once make us see this Father, and we'll be happy!" He understood that this word overturned the normal way people view themselves, went to the root of everything and embraced the horizon of everything, because the Father is the horizon of everything, the root of everything, infinitely more than the closest comparison we can make, that of a child just conceived, for whom the total horizon and the total root is the womb of its mother.
>
> —Servant of God Luigi Giussani
> *La Convenienza Umana della fede* (The Human Convenience of Faith), 127 [translated by Sheila Beatty]

And yet if we have had difficult relationships with our earthly parents, talk of a heavenly Father can sometimes cause us to hesitate. Understandably so. For when we were children the actions of our parents provided the only model we had for understanding the nature of God. When, however, the Son of God took on our human nature, he showed us the true nature of God. We could *see* him for who he truly was.

> He who has seen me has seen the Father.
>
> —*John 14:9*

But he did more than that. Christ made it possible for us to become sons and daughters of the Father. Through the gift of the Holy Spirit, we are united to Christ and thereby "born again." We become the sons and daughters of God.

> God has sent the Spirit of his Son into our hearts, crying, "Abba! Father!"
>
> —*Galatians 4:6*

> We know that the whole creation has been groaning with labor pains together until now; and not only the creation, but we ourselves, who have the first fruits of the Spirit, groan inwardly as we await for adoption as sons. . . . Likewise the Spirit helps

> us in our weakness; for we do not know how to pray as we ought, but the Spirit himself intercedes for us with sighs too deep for words.
>
> —*Romans 8:22–23, 26*

In the midst of the persisting insecurity we may feel as a result of the loss of our childhood home and more crucially, the "home" of our parents' mutual love, Jesus invites us to a permanent home of his Father's love.

> Let not your hearts be troubled. . . . In my Father's house are many rooms. . . . And when I go and prepare a place for you, I will come again and will take you to myself, that where I am you may be also. . . . If a man loves me, he will keep my word, and my Father will love him, and we will come to him and make our home with him.
>
> —*John 14:1–3, 23*

Jesus fulfills the hope of the homeless.

> Sing to God, sing praises to his name . . . his name is the LORD, exult before him! Father of the fatherless and protector of widows is God in his holy habitation. God gives the desolate a home to dwell in.
>
> —*Psalm 68:4–6*

Do I struggle with the idea of God as Father? Have I ever experienced Jesus's provision for me in response to my prayer?

LEARNING TO SEE: BAPTISM AND THE SIGN OF THE CROSS

The invitation of Jesus to become sons and daughters of "our Father in heaven" is made a reality for us in the Sacrament of Baptism. Through it, the liberating fact of belonging to God acquires its unexpected and definitive depth: adoption as sons and daughters into the household

Pietro della Francesca, *Baptism of Jesus* (1448–1450), The National Gallery of Art, Washington, DC

of God. St. Basil said that the "words spoken when I received the grace of adoption are more honorable than any spoken since" (*On the Holy Spirit*, 26). At the moment of our death, the Church will recall our Baptism as the most decisive aspect of our lives.

> In the waters of baptism N. died with Christ and rose with him to new life. May he/she now share with him eternal glory.
>
> —*The Funeral Liturgy*
> Roman Ritual

To become ever more aware of our deepest belonging through the rebirth of Baptism, the Church invites us to make the Sign of the Cross. This small gesture is no small thing. In the words of then Cardinal Ratzinger, the Sign of the Cross is no less than the "summing up and re-acceptance of baptism" (*The Spirit of the Liturgy*, 178). Every time we make the Sign of the Cross over ourselves, we *learn to see* the fact that we have been claimed by Another, that we belong to the family of a loving Father. And in the simple gesture of tracing the cross over our body, we are reminded of the safe refuge that we have in his Son, because of the power of his resurrection to transform every dead thing in our lives. Despite the pain, insecurity, anger and grief that we may have as a consequence of our parents' divorce, the Sign of the Cross is a reminder that it is not the losses and betrayals we have suffered that ultimately define us. Baptism does.

In the Name of the Father and of the Son and of the Holy Spirit.

Let us, then, *learn to see* more deeply what we are by reclaiming this simple, yet profound gesture. Here is a word of advice from another great teacher, Romano Guardini:

> When we cross ourselves, let it be with a real Sign of the Cross. Instead of a small, cramped gesture that gives no notion of its meaning, let us make a large unhurried sign, from forehead to breast, from shoulder to shoulder, consciously feeling how it includes the whole of us, our thoughts, our attitudes, our body and soul, every part of us at once.
>
> —Romano Guardini
> *Sacred Signs*, 13

SESSION III

"Hallowed Be Thy Name"

The glory of God is man fully alive.
St. Irenaeus

PRAYER

Opening

L: Lord, open my lips.

R: And my mouth will proclaim your praise.

L: Almighty God, every good thing comes from you. Trusting in your providential care, we ask that you fill our hearts with love for you, increase our faith, and by your constant care protect the good you have given us. We ask this through Christ our Lord. Amen.

Psalm 34:1–18

L: In Psalm 34, the psalmist exalts the name of the Lord because he hears the cry of the poor and comes near to the brokenhearted.

L: I will bless the LORD at all times; his praise shall continually be in my mouth.

R: My soul makes its boast in the LORD; let the humble hear and be glad.

L: O magnify the LORD with me, and let us exalt his name together!

R: I sought the LORD, and he answered me, and delivered me from all my fears.

L: Look to him, and be radiant; so your faces shall never be ashamed.

R: This poor man cried, and the LORD heard him, and saved him out of all his troubles.

L: The angel of the LORD encamps around those who fear him, and delivers them.

R: O taste and see that the LORD is good! Blessed is the man who takes refuge in him!

L: O fear the LORD, you his saints, for those who fear him have no want!

R: The young lions suffer want and hunger; but those who seek the LORD lack no good thing.

L: Come, O sons, listen to me, I will teach you the fear of the LORD.

R: What man is there who desires life, and covets many days, that he may enjoy good?

L: Keep your tongue from evil, and your lips from speaking deceit.

R: Depart from evil, and do good; seek peace, and pursue it.

L: The eyes of the LORD are toward the righteous, and his ears toward their cry.

R: The face of the LORD is against evildoers, to cut off the remembrance of them from the earth.

L: When the righteous cry for help, the LORD hears, and delivers them out of all their troubles.

R: The LORD is near to the brokenhearted, and saves the crushed in spirit.

Reading

Reader:

A Reading from Exodus (3:1–6, 13–14)

Now Moses was keeping the flock of his father-in-law, Jethro, the priest of Midian; and he led his flock to the west side of the wilderness, and came to Horeb, the mountain of God. And the angel of the LORD appeared to him in a flame of fire out of the midst of a bush; and he looked, and behold, the bush was burning, yet it was not consumed. And Moses said, "I will turn aside and see this great sight, why the bush is not burnt." When the LORD saw that he turned aside to see, God called to him out of the bush, "Moses, Moses!" And he said, "Here am I." Then he said, "Do not come near; put off your shoes from your feet, for the place on which you are standing is holy ground." And he said, "I am the God of your father, the God of Abraham, the God of Isaac, and the God of Jacob." . . . Then Moses said to God, "If I come to the sons of Israel and say to them, 'The God of your fathers has sent me to you,' and they ask me, 'What is his name?' what shall I say to them?" God said to Moses, "I AM WHO AM." And he said, "Say this to the sons of Israel, 'I AM has sent me to you.'"

(Prayer in Silence)

Petitions

L: St. Peter Chrysologus said: "We ask God to hallow his name, which by its own holiness saves and makes holy all creation. . . . It is the name that gives salvation to a lost world. But we ask that this name of God should be hallowed in us through our actions. For God's name is blessed when we live well. . . . We ask then that, just as the name of God is holy, we may obtain his holiness in our souls" (Sermo, 71, 4, cited in the CCC, 2814).

L: For minds and hearts turned more easily toward our Father, we ask:

R: Lord, bless us and bring us close to you.

L: For the grace to praise his name always, we ask:

R: Lord, bless us and bring us close to you.

L: For the certainty of his nearness to us, especially when we are broken hearted, we ask:

R: Lord, bless us and bring us close to you.

L: That his love be radiant in us, for the sake of the Church and of the whole world, we ask:

R: Lord, bless us and bring us close to you.

Closing Prayer

L: Heavenly Father, watch over your family who know that in your mercy and loving kindness, no thought of ours is left unguarded, no tear unheeded, no joy unnoticed. May the blessings promised to the poor in spirit lead us to the treasures of your heavenly kingdom, through our Lord, Jesus Christ, your Son, who lives and reigns with you, in the unity of the Holy Spirit, God, forever and ever.

L: Let us call on the name of the Father, who always takes care of his children.

All: Our Father who art in heaven. . . .

L: Glory be to the Father and to the Son and to the Holy Spirit.

R: As it was in the beginning, is now and ever shall be, world without end. Amen.

REFLECTION

In our last session we began to reflect on what is ours through Baptism: a new sharing in Jesus' relation to His Father—whom we now dare to call *Our* Father. But who is this Father? How can we know him and come close to him? How can we discover his love for us? Today we meditate on the first of seven petitions of the Our Father: "Hallowed be thy name." This petition focuses on God himself, on drawing near to him. This is the first and most important goal of the Our Father, indeed of the whole Christian life.

> Nothing can turn out right if our relation to God is not rightly ordered. For this reason, the Our Father begins with God and then, from that starting point, shows us the way toward being human.
>
> —Pope Benedict XVI
> *Jesus of Nazareth*, 134

By seeking a deeper relation to God our Father, we entrust our past, present, and future to him.

Purifying our Image of God

"Hallowed be thy name" invites us to think more deeply about who God is. It invites us to continue to purify our images of God to see his face more clearly so that we can enjoy a relationship with him based who he truly is. Our own experiences of family, especially of our parents, is marked by disorder. When parents divorce, children are often overlooked by parents who are now preoccupied with their own problems. In some cases, they are completely abandoned by one of the parents. Experiences like this can cloud our vision of who God is. We may see *him* as rejecting, abandoning, uninterested, unresponsive, or untrustworthy. Indeed, for this very reason, we may avoid the very idea of a father. With the Our Father we are invited to go beyond these broken images to encounter God as he is and makes himself known.

Do I find myself struggling against a "god" who rejects me, abandons me? What negative or inadequate images of God do I struggle with? As a result of these images of God, in what ways am I open or closed to God?

Michael O'Brien, *Jesus Promises Paradise to the Repentant Thief* (2008), location unknown; Permission granted by artist

God Is Holy—Set Apart

A name signifies who someone is. "Hallowed be Thy Name" calls to mind the encounter between Moses and the Lord who appeared to him in the burning bush. When, with fear and trembling, Moses asked his name, God said: "I AM WHO AM" (*Exodus* 3:14). With this mysterious name God revealed himself as the One who exists from all eternity. This is what sets him apart. He is, as the *Catechism* says, "infinitely above everything we can understand or say" (*CCC*, 206). In this sense, then he is "holy."

Holy, holy, holy is the Lord God Almighty, who was and is and is to come!

—*Revelation 4:8*

God Is Holy—Near to Us

With the petition "Hallowed be thy name," however, we say even more. We express our desire and expectation that we be drawn into God's holiness, a reality which we have already begun to experience in Baptism.

> Asking the Father that his name be made holy draws us into his plan of loving kindness for the fullness of time, "according to his purpose which he set forth in Christ," that we might "be holy and blameless before him in love."
>
> —*CCC, 2807*

Yes, God is above us and greater than us, but he is, for this same reason, close to us. As our Creator he is, as St. Augustine said, "more intimate to me than I am to myself" (*Confessions*, III, 6, 11). Then too, he drew near to us in a new way when he *gave* his name. That began at the burning bush and reached a peak when the Son of God became Man and revealed the "Father." "No one knows the Father except the Son" (*Matthew* 11:27).

> A name expresses a person's essence and identity and the meaning of this person's life. God has a name; he is not an anonymous force. To disclose one's name is to make oneself known to others; in a way it is to hand oneself over by becoming accessible, capable of being known more intimately and addressed personally.
>
> —*CCC, 203*

We could add, too, that in being drawn into the Father's love through his name, we are drawn into life itself and the source of *our lives.*

> The one who stands in the name of God, is immersed in God, is alive, because God—says the Lord—is not a God of the dead, but of the living.
>
> —Benedict XVI
> *Lectio Divina,* June 11, 2012

When we say, "Hallowed be thy name," then, we acknowledge the great gift that the Father has given us in making himself known to us, *as he truly is*: the Father, source of all life. This is particularly important for those of us who live in the wake of divorce, since we may have projected the broken relations we know all too well onto him, and as a consequence, distanced ourselves from him. But it is not our parents who are the measure of God. On the contrary, it is God who is their measure.

> I bow my knees before the Father, from whom every family in heaven and on earth is named.
>
> —*Ephesians 3:14–15*

But how can we encounter this love, this love that was offered to Christ's disciples so many years ago? How, that is, can we really know God by his full name: Father? We do so by "remaining" in the Son, through his Church—through prayer and the sacraments, and vital friendships with others who belong to Christ, our brothers and sisters. The path is simple, even if at times, we must struggle to remain. On that path we will begin to see, in others and in ourselves, the fundamental goodness of life even when marked by imperfection and suffering. We will begin to experience, too, new possibilities: the love for a spouse even when he or she is "no longer lovable," the capacity to sacrifice oneself for others and for one's children, and the very desire to have children. We will begin to see, that is, a humanity fully alive, where God is becoming "everything to everyone" (*1 Corinthians* 15:28). How precious will that be, especially to us!

Do I see evidence of the "nearness" of God? Does it change anything in the way I look at God? Does it change anything in the way I look at myself and others?

LEARNING TO SEE: PRAYER BEFORE THE BLESSED SACRAMENT—ADORATION

When we come before Jesus in the Blessed Sacrament, we *remain* with him and with his Father, our Father. When we remain with Jesus, we accustom our "eyes" to see that the One to whom we ultimately belong has made himself known to us, has drawn near to us, and remains with us.

There, in that place of "co-remaining," we also give Jesus an opportunity to calm our anger, console our grief, and heal our wounds, just as he did in his earthly life. He healed many whom he encountered: St. Peter's mother-in-law, the man born blind, the hemorrhaging woman, and many others. Jesus knows everything that has brought us to this point in our lives better than we do. And he will, with his Father, give us good gifts—above all the gift of himself. All we have to do is open wide our hearts to him so that he can give them to us.

During adoration, we can begin opening our hearts to Jesus spontaneously by simply verbalizing our fears and difficulties to him, then begging for what we need, confident that he knows us in detail—even the "hairs on our head"—and knows exactly what we need and when we need it. This period of opening our hearts to Jesus can give way to meditative prayer. We can read Scripture or pray the Rosary, or simply remain silent—*resting* or *gazing*. All that we really need to do is *be* with him. It is enough that we are there.

Andrei Rublev, *The Trinity* (1410), Tretiakov Gallery, Moscow, Russia

SESSION IV

"Thy Kingdom Come, Thy Will Be Done on Earth as It Is in Heaven"

The Lord is my light and my salvation.
Psalm 27:1

PRAYER

Opening

L: Lord, open my lips.

R: And my mouth will proclaim your praise.

L: Lord our God, we bless you. As we come together to ponder Scriptures, we ask you in your kindness to fill us with the knowledge of your will so that, pleasing you in all things, we may grow in every good work. We ask this through Christ our Lord.

R: Amen.

Catholic Household Blessings and Prayers, National Conference of Catholic Bishops Washington, D.C.: United States Catholic Conference, Inc, 1988, 284.

Psalm 27

L: In Psalm 27, the psalmist expresses his confidence that he will dwell in the Lord's house.

L: The Lord is my light and my salvation; whom shall I fear? The Lord is the stronghold of my life; of whom shall I be afraid?

R: The Lord is my light and my salvation.

L: When evildoers assail me, to devour my flesh, my adversaries and foes, they shall stumble and fall. Though a host encamp against me, my heart shall not fear; though war arise against me, yet I will be confident.

R: The Lord is my light and my salvation.

L: One thing I have asked of the Lord, that will I seek after; that I may dwell in the house of the Lord all the days of my life, to behold the beauty of the Lord, and to inquire in his temple.

R: The Lord is my light and my salvation.

L: For he will hide me in his shelter in the day of trouble; he will conceal me under the cover of his tent, he will set me high upon a rock.

R: The Lord is my light and my salvation.

L: And now my head shall be lifted up above my enemies round about me; and I will offer in his tent sacrifices with shouts of joy; I will sing and make melody to the Lord. Hear, O Lord, when I cry aloud, be gracious to me and answer me!

R: The Lord is my light and my salvation.

L: You have said, "Seek my face." My heart says to you, "Your face, Lord, do I seek." Hide not your face from me. Turn not your servant away in anger, you who have been my help. Cast me not off, forsake me not, O God of my salvation! For my father and my mother have forsaken me, but the Lord will take me up.

R: The Lord is my light and my salvation.

L: Teach me your way, O Lord; and lead me on a level path because of my enemies. Give me not up to the will of my adversaries; for false witnesses have risen against me, and they breathe out violence.

R: The Lord is my light and my salvation.

L: I believe that I shall see the goodness of the Lord in the land of the living!
Wait for the Lord; be strong, and let your heart take courage; yes, wait for the Lord!

R: The Lord is my light and my salvation.

Reading

Reader:
A Reading from Isaiah (49:15)

"Can a woman forget her sucking child, that she should have no compassion on the son of her womb? Even these may forget, yet I will not forget you."

(Prayer in Silence)

Closing Prayer

L: All of our prayers are made perfect and complete in the prayer that Jesus taught us. Let us pray together:

All: Our Father who art in heaven. . . .

L: Glory be to the Father and to the Son and to the Holy Spirit.

R: As it was in the beginning, is now and ever shall be, world without end. Amen.

REFLECTION

Today we look at the next two petitions of the Lord's Prayer: "Thy kingdom come" and "Thy will be done on earth, as it is in heaven." Here, we are seeking God's kingdom and his will for us. Looking at the simple pronoun at the beginning of each of these petitions, we notice first of all that we are asking for *his* kingdom to come and *his* will to be done.

> Seek first his kingdom and his righteousness, and all these things shall be yours as well.
>
> —*Matthew 6:33*

We are placed immediately in a stance of trust before God, so that he might "reign." This is a stance of no small significance for many of us who have reasons to be wary of trust.

What exactly is the "kingdom of God"? Scripture tells us that this kingdom is "righteousness and peace and joy in the Holy Spirit" (*Romans* 14:17). But this "righteousness and peace" is not mere tranquility, or being "left alone." Rather it is the fulfillment of the "plan for the fullness of time, to unite all things in [Christ], things in heaven and things on earth" (*Ephesians* 1:10). The kingdom is a *communion*, a communion with God in Jesus Christ. We can even say that Jesus *is* the kingdom of God, so that to say, "Thy kingdom come" is the same as saying, "Come, Lord Jesus" (*Revelation* 22:20).

> Jesus is the Kingdom of God in person. The Kingdom of God is present wherever he is present. . . . To pray for the Kingdom of God is to say to Jesus: Let us be yours, Lord! Pervade us, live in us; gather scattered humanity in your body, so that in you everything may be subordinated to God and you can then hand over the universe to the Father, in order that "God may be all in all" (*1 Corinthians* 15:28).
>
> —Pope Benedict XVI
> *Jesus of Nazareth*, 146–147

Moreover, though we ask for the Kingdom to "come"—it has already begun. Beginning with the Incarnation of the Son over two thousand years ago, and through his presence in the Church continuing in history to this day, the kingdom is already here, since Christ has already begun to unite things in heaven and things on earth.

> The kingdom of God is in your midst.
>
> —*Luke 17:21*

Why then does the kingdom still have to "come"? It is a matter of a seed planted that still has to grow, to be accomplished in us.

> The life of this Kingdom is Christ's continuing life in those who are his own. . . . In the heart that is touched and transformed by it, the Kingdom begins. . . . The roots of the indestructible tree seek to penetrate into each heart.
>
> —Reinhold Schneider
> *Das Vaterunser*, cited by Pope Benedict XVI
> *Jesus of Nazareth*, 147

But what is it about Christ that he and those united to him are a "kingdom"? It is because he is the One who has done the will of the Father.

> My food is to do the will of him who sent me, and to accomplish his work.
>
> —*John 4:34*

> Jesus' whole existence is summed up in the words "yes, I have come to do thy will."
>
> —Benedict XVI
> *Jesus of Nazareth*, 150

And what is that will? Here, we are not talking about the arbitrary commands of a tyrant. Rather we are talking about the "mysterious will" of a God, who, before the foundation of the world, willed to "unite all things in him, things in heaven and things on earth" (*Romans* 1:4–10), to make us his adopted sons and daughters in his Son (*Romans* 8:29). Thus, when we pray to the Father, "Thy kingdom come. Thy will be done," we are *looking to Christ* and asking that the new life that has begun in us be brought to completion.

> I am sure that he who began a good work in you will bring it to completion at the day of Jesus Christ.
>
> —*Philippians 1:6*

Marriage, Family, and the Kingdom

In a unique way, relations in marriage and the family are caught up with this communion, with God in Jesus Christ. God instituted marriage between man and woman at creation (*Genesis* 1:27–28) and he deemed it "very good" (*Genesis* 1:31). This marriage was filled with peace and harmony.

> The man and his wife were both naked, and were not ashamed.
>
> —*Genesis 2:25*

The first mention of any conflict was not until after the serpent tempted Adam and Eve to disobey God's command not to eat any fruit from the tree of knowledge. Key to understanding the heart of this event is that it begins with disfiguring the image of God by misrepresenting his command:

> Did God say, "You shall not eat of *any* tree in the garden"?
>
> —*Genesis 3:1*

The Tempter insinuates doubt about the goodness of God. ("God wants us to starve!") The taking of the fruit, then, is the consequence of that doubt. It is a *taking for oneself,* since God cannot be trusted to give what is needed.

> *Original sin attempts . . . to abolish fatherhood*, destroying its rays which permeate the created world, placing in doubt the truth about God who is Love and leaving man only with a sense of the master-*slave* relationship. As a result, the Lord appears jealous of his power over the world and over man; and consequently, man feels goaded to do battle against God.
>
> —St. John Paul II
> *Crossing the Threshold of Hope*, 227–228

After eating the fruit, the first man and woman became afraid; they were ashamed of their nakedness because now *their* communion was broken (*Genesis* 3:1–13). From this point on, the lives of man and woman would be marked with suffering, and their relationship would be a struggle (*Genesis* 3:16). But this discord was not the original word on marriage and the family, nor would it be the final word.

Later in Scripture, we read that God chose Israel from among all nations to be his own, in a "covenant." The prophets of the Old Testament expressed this covenant with Israel through the language of fatherhood, childhood, and marriage. For example, the prophet Hosea describes Israel as a child:

> When Israel was a child, I loved him, and out of Egypt I called my son.
>
> —*Hosea 11:1*

Then the prophet Isaiah portrays Israel as a spouse:

> For the LORD delights in you, and your land shall be married. For as a young man marries a virgin, so shall your sons marry you, and as the bridegroom rejoices over the bride, so shall your God rejoice over you.
>
> —*Isaiah 62:4–5*

When referring to Israel as "bride," Isaiah has the occasion to say something about the exceptional character of the divine "Bridegroom." He calls Israel "my delight" *after* her many infidelities—after she has become "forsaken," and "desolate" (*Isaiah* 62:4). God's desire for his "bride" and his fidelity toward her is beyond any human measure.

Then, in the fullness of time, God sent his Son, the "Bridegroom." He would show his limitless fidelity for the "Bride," the Church, when he laid his life down for her on the Cross. It was in doing precisely this—in doing the "will of the Father" unto death—that Christ definitively inaugurated the "kingdom," the "New Covenant." The essence of the New Covenant is Christ's life and love, poured out for his Bride, the Church. As Cardinal Marc Ouellet says:

> God's covenant with Israel and humanity is a story of a wedding. . . . A God who is Bridegroom seeks after his unfaithful bride,

> he regenerates her in the suffering of humbled love, and lifts her up in his glory. The Father sends his Son as a Bridegroom, accompanied by the Holy Spirit, who prepares the bride [the Church] for the encounter with the Bridegroom and the fulfillment of the eschatological wedding.
>
> —Marc Ouellet
> *Divine Likeness*, 80–81

It was in light of *his* wedding, the "wedding of the Lamb" (*Revelation* 19:7) that Christ shed light on marriage itself. When the Pharisees asked Jesus about divorce, he turned them back to "the beginning," to creation, saying:

> Have you not read that he who made them from the beginning made them male and female, and said, "For this reason a man shall leave his father and mother and be joined to his wife, and the two shall become one"? So they are no longer two but one. What therefore God has joined together, let no man put asunder.
>
> —*Matthew 19:46*

It was because of the "hardness of hearts" that the indissoluble "yes" of love had become "impossible," Jesus said. But it had always belonged to marriage since the beginning (see *Matthew* 19:8). And now it is possible again, because spouses are caught up into Christ's faithful love for the Church, through the grace of Baptism and the Sacrament of Marriage. This is why St. Paul instructs husbands and wives to love each other *as* Christ has loved them (*Ephesians* 5:21–33). In this way marriage has come into its own.

Am I able to perceive the truth of marriage,
even through the experience of divorce?
Do I see glimpses of a new Love inside human love?

◀ Pablo Picasso, *The Lovers* (1923), The National Gallery of Art, Washington, DC

Broken Images

When we pray, "Thy will be done on earth, as it is in heaven," we pray for God's will in every aspect of our lives. However, believing in God's will for marriage is a particular challenge for those of us who have been affected by divorce.

> If the most important relationship in your life, which of course is the one with your parents, is irretrievably broken at a young age, and one of the defining components of your life is that that core relationship was not there, you have to have fundamental trust issues.
>
> —Elizabeth Marquardt
> *Between Two Worlds*, 149

Our families have been split in two in many cases because of the infidelity of one or both spouses. And just as fidelity in marriage permits the enduring fidelity of God to shine forth into the world, the experience of infidelity casts a shadow on that same fidelity, and the possibility that it shines in our earthly loves going forward. Even if each one of our parents continues to love and care for us—very much—it is the rift *between* our parents that casts a shadow on the love that "bears all things, believes all things, hopes all things, endures all things . . . [and] never ends" (*1 Corinthians* 13:7–8). If love appears to be so untrustworthy, how then can we entrust ourselves to it—to God's "will" for it?

Due to our experience, we question the possibility of a love that is *forever*. Yet it is this same experience that unearths a deep desire within us. As one child of divorce said,

> I have discovered through all the pain that my desire for my parents to stay together is a desire for the indissolubility of love. My suffering is a testament to the way love should be—forever.
>
> —Anonymous

René Magritte, *The Lovers* (1928), Museum of Modern Art (MoMA), New York, NY; © 2020 C. Herscovici / Artists Rights Society (ARS), New York, NY; Digital Image © The Museum of Modern Art / Licensed by SCALA / Art Resource, New York, NY

Suffering is a boundary experience between two realities in our lives. It makes us aware of evil and wounds us, but it also reveals what we most deeply desire—to love and be loved irrevocably.

Is my own suffering a boundary experience for me? Can I relate to what the child of divorce said above about his suffering?

"Thy Will Be Done" in Human Love

As we have said, God's will for human love is that it be faithful and fruitful, in the image of God's own love for us. Love requires a total, mutual self-giving and receiving. But this is challenging for adult children of divorce. We have not seen this love. As the philosopher Allan Bloom says,

> Children who have gone to the school of conditional relationships should be expected to view the world in light of what they have learned.
>
> —Allan Bloom
> *The Closing of the American Mind*, 119

As a result of our "schooling," we are not primed for mutual self-giving and receiving. On the contrary, we are prone to self-protection. What must we do?

Has my parents' divorce "taught" me that relationships are conditional?

"On Earth, as It Is in Heaven": Witness to a New Fidelity

Praying for God's will in our love goes beyond our wills and capacities alone. When we pray "Thy kingdom come. Thy will be done on earth, as it is in heaven," we pray as those who have already been brought into the "kingdom" of the Son, namely *the Church*, his Bride, the object of his faithful love. As St. Augustine said:

> It would not be inconsistent with the truth to understand the words, "Thy will be done on earth as it is in heaven," to mean: "in the Church as in our Lord Jesus Christ himself"; or "in the Bride who has been betrothed, just as in the Bridegroom who has accomplished the will of the Father."
>
> —St. Augustine
> *De Serm. Dom.* 2, 6, 24, cited in the *CCC*, 2827

Thus, when we pray "Thy kingdom come. Thy will be done," we must continually attach ourselves to the Church. It is there that the memory of Christ's fidelity to the Father and to his bride can be kept alive in us, because it is there that we can experience this gift continually, in the Church's sacraments, liturgical life, common life, and teachings. It is there too that his fidelity to the Church can be accomplished *in us* and in our marriages, present or hoped for: "on earth, as it is in heaven."

LEARNING TO SEE: SCRIPTURAL MEDITATION

Meditation on Scripture every day is a privileged way to discover Christ and his will for our lives. This session's practice is to meditate on a passage of Scripture using a style similar to the one used by St. Ignatius in his famous work, *The Spiritual Exercises*. In particular we propose the account of the *Wedding Feast of Cana* because it helps us to see the "newness" that Christ brings to life and to marriage.

General Instructions for a Scriptural Meditation

1. Read the Scripture passage.
2. Read the Scripture a second time.
3. Close your eyes. Imagine the scene. Place yourself in the position of someone in the passage. Use your five senses to imagine the scene around you throughout this meditation.
4. Relate the biblical account to your life in all of its particularity.
5. Recall words in the Scripture, especially Christ's words. Let them speak to you in this moment of your life.

The Wedding of Cana: John 2:1–11

On the third day there was a marriage at Cana in Galilee, and the mother of Jesus was there; Jesus was also invited to the marriage, with his disciples. When the wine failed, the mother of Jesus said to him, "They have no wine." And Jesus said to her, "O woman, what have you to do with me? My hour has not yet come." His mother said to the servants, "Do whatever he tells you." Now six stone jars were standing there, for the Jewish rites of purification, each holding twenty or thirty gallons. Jesus said to them, "Fill the jars with water." And they filled them up to the brim. He said to them, "Now draw some out, and take it to the steward of the feast." So they took it. When the steward of the feast tasted the water now become wine, and did not know where it came from (though the servants who had drawn the water knew), the steward of the feast called the bridegroom and said to him, "Every man serves the good wine first; and when men have drunk freely, then the poor wine; but you have kept the good wine until now." This, the first of his signs, Jesus did at Cana in Galilee, and manifested his glory; and his disciples believed in him.

1. Read the passage.

2. Read the passage again.

3–5. Close your eyes and visualize the scene; relate the account to your life; let the words of Scripture speak to you.

(Pause)

- What are you seeing as you take the place of the bridegroom, or the bride who is by his side? What are your surroundings? Do you hear laughter and sounds of joy all around you at the feast? Is there music? Are you excited that you have entered into holy marriage? What are the smells in the air? Do you taste the food or sip the wine that is in front of you? Do you see your beautiful spouse? What is he or she wearing?

(Pause)

- Like the bridegroom, you are anxious about the wine running out. Wine represents the joy of life, the joy of love. Perhaps your "wine" too has run out, because of your parents' divorce. Do you feel dry and empty like the wineskin that held the wine?

(Pause)

- Recall now a bad experience you have had in a dating relationship or in your marriage, one that might have been in some way connected to your parents' divorce. Perhaps you were afraid of becoming too close. Perhaps you were making the same mistake your parents did. Perhaps you thought that love could not last forever. Whatever it was, recall it now.

(Pause)

- Our Mother Mary now comes to your assistance like she did at the Wedding Feast of Cana. She is moved by your sorrow. She turns to Christ, who is there with her, visibly moved with compassion. She asks Christ for a new wine, a new joy for your life. Do you see them gazing lovingly at you, and speaking about a new wine for you?

(Pause)

- At first, Christ's response is jarring: "Woman, what have you to do with me? My hour has not yet come." Doesn't Christ care about you? Doesn't he care about us? Perhaps there is no new wine in life. Yet then you hear Mary's last words to us in Scripture: "Do whatever he tells you." She understands the true meaning of Christ's words. She knows that his question—"What have you to do with me?"—is not a lack of sympathy but an invitation to faith. Mary responds with a perfect act of faith, "Do whatever he tells you." Can we hear these same words spoken by Mary to us? "Do whatever he tells you." What is your response? Will you believe in Christ's power to give you every good thing?

(Pause)

- After this moment, Christ takes water used for Jewish purification rites for marriage and turns it into wine. By this surprising act, Christ is bringing a new joy to our lives by transforming marriage into something unfathomably beautiful and holy. He is making it *new* (a new "wine"). Married love now carries his presence, and because of his presence, that love is capable of remaining faithful to the end. This wine of Christ's love is ultimately poured out for the Church on the Cross and made sacramentally present in the Eucharist. Both lift marriage up and safeguard and strengthen it in the face of sin and brokenness. Taste therefore this wine that the headwaiter brings to you on behalf of Christ. What does it taste like? Is it sweet, semi-sweet, or dry?

(Pause)

- You are astonished at the quality of this wine. It is unlike anything you have ever tasted before. You look at your spouse with a smile. There is something new here now. The headwaiter says to you, "Everyone serves the good wine first and then when people have drunk freely, an inferior one; but you have kept the good wine until now." Now with a smile, together you and your spouse drink some more. It is so good, so *pure*. It refreshes your lips and mouth, parched dry from the joylessness from your parents' divorce. As you take another sip of wine, feel this new indissoluble love of Christ entering every part of your body—your veins, your hands, your head, and your heart.

(Pause)

- Then with your spouse beside you, you hold the chalice of this new wine together. You do not need to ask the headwaiter where it came from. You both know. You look to Christ, and he looks at you. He raises his hands, lays them upon you, and blesses you. Love now lasts forever not because it has been freed from all mistakes or weaknesses, but because your love is in his hands. You begin to believe in this new love, like the disciples at Cana began to believe in Christ. Christ embraces you. You can hear his heartbeat. With every beat it says, "I love you." "I love you." "I love you." Stay there as long as you wish and know that you are Christ's beloved.[1]

1 Adapted from a meditation written by Daniel Meola, co-founder and president of Life-Giving Wounds.

SESSION V

"Give Us This Day Our Daily Bread"

"Give us": the trust of children who look to their Father for everything is beautiful.
CCC, 2828

PRAYER

Opening

L: Lord, open my lips.

R: And my mouth shall proclaim your praise.

Psalm 104:1–2, 13–15, 24, 27–28

L: In Psalm 104, the psalmist blesses the Lord because he gives food in due season.

L: Bless the Lord, O my soul! O Lord my God, you are very great! You are clothed with honor and majesty, who cover yourself with light as with a garment, who have stretched out the heavens like a tent.

R: Bless the Lord, my soul.

L: From your lofty abode you water the mountains; the earth is satisfied with the fruit of your work.

R: Bless the Lord, my soul.

L: You cause grass to grow for the cattle, and plants for man to cultivate, that he may bring forth food from the earth, and wine to gladden the heart of man, oil to make his face shine, and bread to strengthen man's heart.

R: Bless the Lord, my soul.

L: O Lord, how manifold are your works! In wisdom you have made them all; the earth is full of your creatures.

R: Bless the Lord, my soul.

L: These all look to you, to give them their food in due season. When you give to them, they gather it up; when you open your hand, they are filled with good things.

R: Bless the Lord, my soul.

Reading

Reader:
A reading from the Gospel of John (4:31–34)

Meanwhile the disciples begged him, saying "Rabbi, eat." But he said to them, "I have food to eat of which you do not know." So the disciples said to one another, "Has any one brought him food?" Jesus said to them, "My food is to do the will of him who sent me, and to accomplish his work."

Reflection

L: St. Teresa of Avila wrote:
This bread . . . is ours daily . . . because we have him here on earth, since he has remained with us here and we receive him; and, if we profit by his company, we shall also have him in heaven, for the only reason he remains with us is to help and encourage and sustain us so that we shall do that will, which . . . is to be fulfilled in us.

St. Teresa of Avila, *The Way of Perfection*, chapter 33

(Prayer in Silence)

Response

L: I have food to eat of which you do not know.

R: I have food to eat of which you do not know.

L: My food is to do the will of the one who sent me.

R: I have food to eat of which you do not know.

Petitions

L: For those who toil to earn their daily bread:

R: Lord, we pray.

L: For those without work or resources:

R: Lord, we pray.

L: That the goods of the earth may be shared among all:

R: Lord, we pray.

L: For the poor and the those who hunger:

R: Lord, we pray.

Closing Prayer

O God, who in this wonderful Sacrament
have left us a memorial of your Passion,
grant us, we pray,
so to revere the sacred mysteries of your Body and Blood
that we may always experience in ourselves
the fruits of your redemption.
Who live and reign with God the Father
in the unity of the Holy Spirit,
God, for ever and ever.

Collect, *The Feast of Corpus Christi*

L: Let us call on the name of the Father, who always takes care of his children.

All: Our Father who art in Heaven. . . .

L: Glory be to the Father and to the Son and to the Holy Spirit.

R: As it was in the beginning, is now and ever shall be, world without end. Amen.

REFLECTION

So far, we have been challenged to lay our sorrows before our Father in heaven and entrust our past to him. Now, we entrust our future, our "daily bread," to God. One of the basic tasks that a father and mother have is to feed their children. At the core of that task is placing the child before the loving goodness of his or her parents. Feeding a child is an expression of goodness.

> Or what man of you, if his son asks him for bread,
> will give him a stone?
>
> —*Matthew 7:9*

It is noteworthy that most infants have their first "meal" in the arms of their mothers—at just the right distance to recognize her face. Then, growing up, children eat *with* those who feed them around a table. The giving of food is a sign of a deeper giving: the presence of the parents themselves to their children and to each other.

The parents themselves are also a sign. When they pray at the table, they point to the One in whom their love for each other is bound, and on whom their very life depends, day by day, moment by moment. They are a sign of the source of all goodness who gives us a life worth sustaining, a life "in abundance" (*John* 10:10). How much of their common work as "primary educators" is caught up in the business of feeding their children and working for their food!

Michael O'Brien, *St. Joseph the Worker* (2006), Victoria, BC, Canada; Permission granted by artist

Anxiety

Ever since the Fall in the Garden of Eden, however, this task has not been easy. As a result of our first parents' distrust that God would give them what they most needed, we all have to toil and labor for our food.

> In the sweat of your face you shall eat bread.
>
> —*Genesis 3:19*

Now we have to suffer the elements in order to eat. This, of course, can be a tremendous source of anxiety. At one time or another, most families find themselves anxious about their next meal, their "daily bread." It can be difficult for parents to provide their children with food in the most literal sense. More difficult still is the provision of the nourishment children most crave: the love that gave them their very lives. Parents must toil to provide that "bread" by drawing on the ultimate Source that sustains their love. The work is well worth it, for when they do so, children are "full."

When parents get divorced, they give up that toil and cease to provide for their children in the deepest sense. However much parents individually manage to get food on the table, in every sense, they are no longer at the table *together*. Now it is the children who are anxious about their "next meal," about what they most want and need "at the table," but what is *not there*. And in its absence, they are anxious too about their future. Can they expect a good and happy future? A life-long and fruitful love?

Jesus knows this anxiety of ours. And he tells us to be anxious no more. But on what basis? And for what reason? Is this just wishful or "positive thinking"? No. His very presence as the Son of the Father is the reason.

> Therefore I tell you, do not be anxious about your life, what you shall eat or what you shall drink. . . . Look at the birds of the air: they neither sow nor reap nor gather into barns, and yet your heavenly Father feeds them. Are you not of more value than they? . . . Therefore do not be anxious, saying "What shall we eat?" or "what shall we drink?" . . . your heavenly Father knows that you need them all. But seek first his kingdom and his righteousness, and all these things shall be yours as well.... Let the day's own trouble be sufficient for the day.
>
> —*Matthew 6:25–26, 31–34*

In putting our most basic needs in God's hands through daily acts of entrustment, we can begin to encounter the One who ultimately sustain us. This is no small matter for those of us who are particularly "hungry."

Anger

When people are "hungry" for love, it is all too natural to become angry. Children of divorce are particularly prone to anger because they have been deprived of the love of their mother and father *together*. Anger arises out of a sorrow over one's pain and a desire to right an injustice (Aquinas, *Summa Theologica,* II-II, q. 158, a. 2). Anger is not wrong in itself, since the desire for justice is not wrong. It becomes wrong, however, when we allow it to become excessive. Anger is also disordered when it causes us to fall away from the true love of neighbor, which includes the one with whom we are angry, the offending party (Aquinas, *Summa,* II-II, q. 158, a. 3). To put it more concretely, anger becomes wrong when we cease to desire our parents' true good. As St. Paul wrote:

> Let everyone speak the truth with his neighbor, for we are members one of another. Be angry but do not sin; do not let the sun go down on your anger, and give no opportunity to the devil.
>
> —*Ephesians 4:25–26*

As with anxiety, when anger arises, we should entrust it to God. We can hand it over in the offering at Mass. When the gifts of bread and wine are presented for the offertory, we can "add" our anger as that part of our humanity we are asking to be transformed. We can make the gifts *heavy* with our humanity in the hope of receiving the "new bread" God wants to give us. At Mass, and in our daily prayer, we can pray for the "daily bread" of a greater love. As Pope Francis said to engaged couples,

> In the prayer of the Our Father we say: "Give us this day our daily bread." Spouses can also learn to pray like this: "Lord, give us this day our daily love," for the daily love of spouses is

> bread, the true bread of the soul, what sustains them in going forward. This is the prayer for engaged couples and spouses. Teach us to love one another, to will good to the other! The more you trust in him, the more your love will be "forever" able to be renewed, and it will conquer every difficulty.
>
> —Pope Francis
> *Address to Engaged Couples on St. Valentine's Day*, 2014

As part of this prayer for the daily bread of love, we can also ask God for guidance in loving those with whom we are angry. We might consider taking time to reflect prayerfully on the sources of our anger, then discuss this with the person(s) or with a trusted advisor. If this fails to bring about a resolution, we may decide to take some distance from the person(s) or situations that give rise to our anger. After several reasonable attempts to amend the situation, we may have to accept things as they are, turn our efforts toward forgiveness of the one who offended us, and surrender our anger to God.

Have I struggled with anger due to my parents' divorce? Are the suggestions above helpful for facing that anger? What else could be helpful?

New Bread

When he was tempted, Christ acknowledged that the food which sustains us is ultimately given by the Father. When Jesus himself was fasting in the wilderness and was tempted by the devil to turn stones into bread, he replied: "Man shall not live by bread alone, but by every word that proceeds from the mouth of God" (*Matthew* 4:4). It was here that he began to introduce his disciples to a new Bread, the Bread for which all other bread is a sign. When the crowd tried to make him king because he had performed the miracle of the multiplication of the loaves and fishes, Jesus admonished them because they were missing the mystery and depth of the sign:

> Do not labor for the food which perishes, but for the food which endures to eternal life.
>
> —*John 6:27*

This "food which endures" and which comes from the Father is Jesus himself, "the Word that comes forth from the mouth of God," the "Word made flesh."

> I am the living bread which came down from heaven; if anyone eats of this bread, he will live forever; and the bread which I shall give for the life of the world is my flesh.
>
> —*John 6:51*

This is why, when Jesus asks us to pray "Give us this day our daily bread," we do not pray in vain. He himself, present before us and in us, is already the response. Here is one testimony from a child of divorce about the importance of Christ's presence in the Eucharist for healing:

> My dad had left our family when I was a senior in high school and my parents' very messy divorce, complete with a giant custody battle over my two youngest brothers, wasn't finalized until the week I graduated college. I struggled those four years, vowing I would never get married and expose myself to such heartache and brokenness again. During my final semester, full of grief, I decided to respond positively to an invitation from a friend to start attending daily Mass.
>
> I was a daily communicant for fifteen years, from my senior year of college until the birth of my first child. When I was engaged and preparing for the Sacrament of Marriage, my fiancé (now husband) and I were both committed to receiving Christ daily because we knew that it was essential to what we were trying to build. While coming from a broken home continues to present its challenges, particularly now as I strive to live out the vocation of marriage, my life is decidedly different. Where there used to be utter despair, depression, anxiety, and doubt, there is still struggle—but also moments of real peace, hope, encouragement, and even joy. I am often reminded of a line

from my favorite book, *Hannah Coulter* by Wendell Berry: "You can't give yourself over to love for somebody without giving yourself over to suffering. . . . It is this body of our suffering that Christ was born into, to suffer it himself and to fill it with light, so that beyond the suffering we can imagine Easter morning and the peace of God."

This is what the Eucharist has been to me. Christ enters my suffering being every time I receive the Eucharist, transforming and healing the wounds with his Love, restoring what has been lost, and providing the grace, strength and desire to be present to this moment. This encounter with Christ gives me the courage to give myself over to love, especially when the wounds of being a child of divorce tempt me into fear. It's not always easy, but the grace is always there, waiting to be at home in me, gently leading me Home.

—Anonymous

*Do I have at least a glimpse
of the presence of Jesus in my life?*

Michelangelo Caravaggio, *Supper at Emmaus* (1601), The National Gallery, London, UK

Our Daily Bread

Finally, we ask for *our* daily bread, not *my* daily bread. Our Father in heaven is the Father of us all. Praying for others' needs as well as our own reminds us that we belong to the human family, and then through Baptism, to the family of the Church. Our belonging to the Church is especially precious to us as children of divorce who have known a very particular and deep loneliness. Our belonging to the Church is as indestructible as our belonging to Christ:

> The cup of blessing which we bless, is it not a participation in the blood of Christ? The bread which we break, is it not a participation in the body of Christ? Because there is one bread, we who are many are one body, for we all partake of the one bread.
>
> —*1 Corinthians 10:16–17*

Our prayer, "Give us this day our daily bread," at once asks for and testifies to this belonging.

LEARNING TO SEE: THE MASS—"OUR DAILY BREAD"

"Give us this day our daily bread." All of us need nourishment to live. As adult children of divorce, we have experienced great want. Even if our material needs were met, all of us experienced the loss of our parents' marriage–of their love for each other–and through that our clarity about God's goodness. Having been deprived of that deeper nourishment, we have become accustomed to "making our own bread," so to speak. As we grow in a new and deeper knowledge of and unity with *our Father*, we will begin to experience his Providence—his provision of what we most need. We are starving for his love; he will not deprive us of it!

The place where we experience this provision above all is in the Mass. There, together with Christ's body, we offer our very selves—hungry and needy—to the Father. In return we receive "our daily bread," the body, blood, soul, and divinity of the Son of God. This session's practice is to take a *deeper look* at the Mass, to see what is given to us: the love of the Father through his Son. Perhaps we can even take advantage of *daily* Mass when we are able.

Fra Angelico, *The Last Supper* (1446), San Marco, Florence, Italy

SESSION VI

"Forgive Us Our Trespasses as We Forgive Those Who Trespass against Us"

Have mercy on me, O God, according to your merciful love.
Psalm 51:1

PRAYER

Opening

L: Hear, O Israel: The Lord our God is one Lord.

R: Therefore, you shall love the Lord your God with all your heart, and with all your soul, and with all your might. (Deuteronomy 6:4–5)

Psalm 103:8–18

L: In Psalm 103, the psalmist offers a prayer of thanksgiving to the God who is rich in mercy.

L: The Lord is merciful and gracious, slow to anger and abounding in mercy.

R: He will not always chide, nor will he keep his anger forever.

L: He does not deal with us according to our sins, nor repay us according to our iniquities.

R: For as the heavens are high above the earth, so great is his mercy toward those who fear him; as far as the east is from the west, so far does he remove our transgressions from us.

L: As a father pities his children, so the Lord pities those who fear him.

R: For he knows our frame; he remembers that we are dust.

L: As for man, his days are like grass; he flourishes like a flower of the field;

R: For the wind passes over it, and it is gone, and its place knows it no more.

L: But the mercy of the Lord is from everlasting to everlasting upon those who fear him,

R: And his righteousness to children's children, to those who keep his covenant and remember to do his commandments.

Closing Prayer

L: Confident that God, our Father, hears all our prayers, we pray the prayer that Jesus taught us.

All: Our Father who art in Heaven. . . .

REFLECTION

This petition of the Lord's Prayer brings us to a crossroads in our journey toward the Father. We have already been asked to lay our past and future down at the feet of Jesus. Moving forward now requires us to forgive those who have trespassed against us. This forgiveness—that seems so difficult, especially for us—is paradoxically the only way to recover our broken origins and rekindle hope for the future. And, of course, as the petition itself suggests, it is the very condition for our own forgiveness.

The Difficulty of Forgiving

As members of the human race, we have been trespassed against by many. The most difficult to forgive are those closest to us: our families, especially our parents. For those of us who have experienced our parents' divorce, it is our mothers and fathers who come to mind when we pray: "forgive those who trespass against us." We have spent years denying that their decision was a "trespass," convincing ourselves (or being told) that it was "all for the best."

But now we have come to see how much of a trespass it was and how many of its effects we bear. We carry many burdens: secrets, divided loyalties, loneliness, abandonment, loss of childhood, precocious adulthood, censorship of feelings, stress during holidays and major life events, and so on. What is more, many of us struggle to believe that enduring love is possible *for us.* Indeed, we have come face-to-face with the reality that our parents' divorce has wounded us at the depths of our being; it has made us essentially homeless, distorting our image of God and of ourselves.

> When their community is not, my being is shaken.
>
> —Andrew Root
> *Children of Divorce,* 86

It is because of the depth of our sorrow that many of us have pushed the pain away, acting as if it did not exist. We have packaged it up and buried it deep behind the closed doors of our hearts. Were we to truly forgive our parents, we would have to look at it squarely in the face. We convinced ourselves long ago that it was better to conceal our grief than to face it. We feared that that if we were to plumb the depths of our sorrow, it would engulf us. *Who would console us anyway? How would we maintain the façade of cordiality and respectfulness?* So we have kept it buried, telling ourselves and others that it does not exist. Yet our hearts increasingly call out to us for freedom. They long to be liberated. We are not exempt from this task: "for freedom Christ has set us free" (*Galatians* 5:1). How then is it possible to forgive our parents?

What have been the greatest obstacles for me in forgiving my parents?

Forgiveness: A New Beginning

The answer to this question requires us first to understand the meaning of forgiveness. To forgive is *not* to excuse or condone an injustice. Nor is it to "just forget it." Damage has been done and we live with its bitter consequences. With forgiveness, rather, we face the injustice head on. We call to mind the precise nature of how we were wronged while deciding to let go of excessive anger, victimhood, indignation, moral superiority, the desire to do the other harm, or the wish for his or her ultimate demise. In its essence, forgiveness means to restore humanity to the ones who have injured us by considering them no longer enemies, but brothers and sisters who share our humanity—our same essential dignity, goodness, and destiny.

For adult children of divorce, forgiveness means to restore humanity to the very ones who gave us our own humanity (together with God). Indeed, in this case, so much is forgiving, *not* forgetting; it is the recalling of their unity. Forgiveness is an interior disposition which is the fruit of a transformation that takes time and effort aided by God's grace. It is the change in the eyes of our hearts, one that allows us to see the other as God sees him or her. Simultaneously, it enables us to *be restored*, since now our hearts are unencumbered, free to love fully. Forgiveness is a gift (for*give*ness) given independent of actual repentance or even of actual reconciliation.

How does this understanding of forgiveness fit with my prior notions? What about it appeals to me? What about it challenges me?

Our Father—Rich in Mercy

Ultimately, for forgiveness to be complete and bear fruit that will last, it must flow from a heart that has encountered the One who is "rich in mercy" (*Ephesians* 2:4). He is the Giver of all gifts, beginning with life itself. All throughout salvation history, God sought out his people and gave them back the unity—with him and with each other—that they had lost through sin. Rather than taking distance from them on account of their betrayal, he drew near to them, conquering them with mercy (*misericordia*), drawing their misery (*miseri-*) into his heart (*-cordia*). In our own personal histories as well, it is the Father who gives back that same unity which we break through our many transgressions.

To peer into the heart of God the Father, we do well to meditate on the figure of the father in the parable of the prodigal son (*Luke* 15:11–32). There we see an image of One who never ceases to look for us when we go astray. We see a God who longs to forgive, eagerly awaiting our return. And when we do return with repentance and contrition and receive his forgiveness, we see a Father who lavishly celebrates our homecoming, by welcoming us back into his household as his beloved sons and daughters. How great is the love and mercy of our God! He is the ever-faithful One, the unfathomable and unsparing source of all love and giving.

God reveals his merciful riches most fully in his Son, Jesus Christ, who assumed our human nature and bore the burden of our guilt, sacrificing himself for the expiation of our sins. In Jesus, the Father makes life spring forth from what was lost and dead through sin. He brings about a "new beginning," a "new creation."

> Therefore, if anyone is in Christ, he is a new creation; the old has passed away; behold, the new has come.
>
> —*2 Corinthians 5:17*

Having encountered the heart of the Father and received the unfathomable gift of his mercy, we cannot keep it for ourselves alone.

God's mercy is so super-abundant and undeserved that it must spill over, cascading from our hearts onto those who have wounded us, even our parents. Only by sinking our roots into that Origin which is deeper than the one we have in our parents can we forgive our parents, "restoring" their humanity with respect to how we look at them. Remaining in *his* love, a love that is stronger than theirs, we can see our parents with the eyes of God the Father and behold their dignity anew.

The Church is an experience of the One who is "rich in mercy." Can I attest to this? How so?

Forgiveness Is Ongoing Because It Is Unconditional

Christ told Peter that forgiveness should be unlimited.

> Then Peter came up and said to [Jesus], "Lord, how often shall my brother sin against me, and I forgive him? As many as seven times?" Jesus said to him, "I do not say to you seven times, but seventy times seven."
>
> —*Matthew 18:21–22*

As children of divorce, we are challenged by limitless forgiveness in a special way since divorce can be a lifelong grief (assuming our parents do not reunite). Indeed, their divorce appears at every new turn in life. But why do we need to forgive again and again? It is because forgiveness is the expression of *unconditional* love. In fact, *just after* Christ offered this teaching about forgiveness, he turned back to "the beginning" and spoke of the indissolubility of marriage. "What therefore God has joined together, let no man put asunder" (*Matthew* 19:6).

In linking these two—forgiveness and marriage—Christ was pointing to the *reason* for forgiving over and over again: an indissoluble love, a love without condition. That love speaks deeply to our hearts as children of divorce, since what we have suffered is precisely the rejection of it. But that also makes forgiveness doubly difficult for us, since it is lifelong and addressed to those who have refused to bestow lifelong forgiveness on each other. And yet with the help of the unfathomable mercy of God, we have an opportunity to break the cycle of our parents' failure to forgive. We can love with the love of Christ who forgave us "while we were yet sinners" (*Romans* 5:8). Like Christ on the Cross—and with him—we can pray for our parents: "Father, forgive them; for they know not what they do" (*Luke* 23:34).

> If we belong to Christ we are not, in the end, determined by divorce, or even by toxic marriages that are as bad as divorce. We do not have to accept the descriptions other human beings impose on us. We can forgive them, for they know not what they do. Even less do they know what they say. . . . [I]n Christ, we can actually give the love we should like to have received ourselves, most especially to those who are tempted to despair. We can be prophets of Hope. "Give and it will be given to you. Good measure, pressed down, shaken together, running over."
>
> —Nicky Rowdon
> "Cold War," *Humanum*

Forgiveness must be carried forward by many interior acts of forgiveness. Only in this way will our emotions fully come in line with our intellect and will. It might be helpful to imagine—without excusing them—what our parents were going through prior to and at the time of their divorce. What was going on inside of them that led them to it? What external pressures or influences may have been acting on them? How did their histories shape them such that they made this choice? As we ponder these things, we can see them for what they are—children of God like us, who are caught up in the cosmic struggle between good and evil, sometimes succumbing to darkness and sometimes victorious in the Light. When we struggle to forgive our parents, we can find greater freedom by sincerely praying for them: "Lord, bless my parents with your love and grace. Help me to see them and forgive them as you do."

Indeed, in order to truly forgive we must recognize that *we too are sinners* in need of mercy. "All have sinned and fall short of the glory of God," St. Paul tells us (*Romans* 3:23). We must therefore pray, "forgive us *our* trespasses, as we forgive those who trespass against us" in order that the good Christ desired for us and our parents can be brought to fulfillment.

Finally, let us recall that in the Our Father, Christ makes our forgiveness of others a condition for our own forgiveness: ". . . *as* we forgive those who trespass against us." Why? It is because if we are not willing to live this unconditional love of Christ, we cannot truly receive his unconditional love for us.

> As we pardon everyone from whom
> We suffer wrong, be kind to pardon us,
> And never look upon what we deserve.
>
> —Dante
> *Purgatorio*, 11.16–18

When have I most experienced the Father's mercy in my life? What do I think of Rowdon's remark, "We can forgive them, for they know not what they do, even less do they know what they say"?

Reconciliation and Boundaries

As we have seen, forgiveness involves a change of heart toward the people who have committed some injustice against us. It involves a decision to let go of hatred, resentment, and superiority, and to invite the Father who is rich in mercy to open our eyes and see our parents as he does. All of this takes place primarily in the interior space of our hearts. Forgiveness *may* lead to reconciliation, the re-uniting of formerly estranged parties in a bond of mutual love and respect.

William Congdon, *Crocifisso n. 2* (1960), Galleria d'Arte Contemporanea of the Pro Civitate Christiana, Assisi, Italy ▶

But unlike the interior transformation of forgiveness, reconciliation requires the involvement and good will of both parties. The ones who are forgiven *receive* forgiveness—recognizing the harmful words and deeds spoken and committed and the damage that they have done—and desire to make amends. Ideally this would include acts of contrition and repentance (though in the case of divorce, parents who persist in divorce are in some sense not capable of full repentance). In reconciliation, the parties work together to restore a relationship in which mutual love and respect can grow. Reconciliation is a difficult but beautiful process that calls for the sincerity, good will, and patience of everyone involved.

Reconciliation, of course, is not always possible or prudent in this life. We have to accept that in "this valley of tears," there can be circumstances that make reconciliation on earth imprudent or even (humanly) impossible. Our parents may not wish to be reconciled. They may not want to receive forgiveness, acknowledging thereby the harm they have done (see *Matthew* 18:15–17). In such cases, we can continue to forgive and love them but with a healthy sense of detachment, entrusting them to the tender love of our Father, but not expecting anything new in return.

Even with reconciliation, however, it may still be necessary to set boundaries in order to prevent ongoing or further harm. There are many good reasons for setting limits on the amount of time we spend with our parents, what we discuss with them, and the degree to which we choose to be involved in their lives and invite them into ours. One such reason is abuse. Reconciliation has nothing to do with tolerating and acquiescing to manipulation, control, disregard, disdain, or contempt. Nor does it have to do with the more subtle abuse of parents turning to their children as their primary source of affection and support, putting them in the place of the spouse. On the contrary, it is entirely compatible with reconciliation (and/or forgiveness), to speak respectfully against these behaviors and to maintain boundaries to avoid them. They are unhealthy and do harm to both children and parents. We do well to identify them and not enable them (for the sake of "peace"). These reasons and many more require us to prayerfully think through what limits we need to maintain in order to love our parents in a way that is healthy for them and for us. *How much of myself can I share with my parents while avoiding resentment and maintaining interior peace? How can I act charitably towards my parents, with a loving, respectful attitude, while also protecting my dignity, my healing, and my vocation, and those of my spouse and my children?* The answers to these questions require prudence, honest self-examination, and often, wise counsel.

It must, of course, be kept in mind that *setting boundaries* is not the same as refusing to suffer offense. Love always entails suffering; it is an inevitable and necessary part of loving finite, fallen human beings. In order to discern the difference between tolerable suffering we choose to endure out of love for another and suffering that we cannot and ought not endure—because of the damage it causes in us and in those causing it—once again, we need to pray for wisdom, and perhaps seek good counsel.

To what extent is true reconciliation with my parents possible for me?

LEARNING TO SEE: BEGINNING TO FORGIVE OUR PARENTS WITH THE DIVINE MERCY CHAPLET

We who have been especially wounded to the core by the betrayal of others face a great challenge. Forgiveness is not easy. We cannot do this alone, especially if we are to forgive in the deepest sense. To be capable of forgiveness, then, we must beg for help from the One who is "rich in mercy" (*Ephesians* 2:4).

In time, as we practice forgiveness, we may discover that we see not only our parents—and others—differently but ourselves as well. Extending forgiveness to others often forces us to appreciate all the more the times when we have been forgiven. Perhaps too, through forgiveness of others, we will discover new ways in which we need forgiveness, ways that were previously hidden to us. The Our Father teaches us this connection between forgiving and being forgiven.

This session's practice is to ask for the grace to forgive our parents, as a participation in God's forgiveness of and mercy on the whole world. In particular, we propose the *Chaplet of Divine Mercy,* a spiritual devotion that developed in the twentieth century based upon the diary of St. Faustina Kowalska. It was recommended by Pope St. John Paul II to the whole Church with the establishment of Divine Mercy Sunday on the Second Sunday of Easter. The Chaplet is centered upon the meditation of Christ's mercy offered on the Cross. As Jesus said to St. Faustina, "Look into My Heart and see there the love and mercy which I have for humankind, and especially for sinners. Look, and enter into My Passion" (*Diary*, entry #1663).

Instructions for How to Pray the Divine Mercy Chaplet

The Divine Mercy Chaplet is prayed using normal rosary beads.

- Begin with the Sign of the Cross.
- Opening Prayer (optional):

> *You expired, Jesus, but the source of life gushed forth for souls, and the ocean of mercy opened up for the whole world. O Fount of Life, unfathomable Divine Mercy, envelop the whole world and empty yourself out upon us.*
>
> Then repeat three times: *O Blood and Water, which gushed forth from the Heart of Jesus as a fountain of Mercy for us, I trust in You!*

- Pray one Our Father, one Hail Mary, and the Apostles' Creed.
- On the Our Father beads pray:

> *Eternal Father, I offer you the Body and Blood, Soul and Divinity of your dearly beloved Son, our Lord Jesus Christ, in atonement for our sins and those of the whole world.*

Image of Divine Mercy; Iconographer: Fr. Pachomius Meade, O.S.B. (2007) ▶

JESUS, I TRUST IN YOU

- On the 10 Hail Mary beads pray:

  For the sake of his sorrowful Passion, have mercy on us and on the whole world.

- Repeat these last two steps for all five decades.
- Conclude by repeating the following prayer three times:

  Holy God, Holy Mighty One, Holy Immortal One, have mercy on us and on the whole world.

- Closing Prayer (optional):

  Eternal God, in whom mercy is endless and the treasury of compassion inexhaustible, look kindly upon us and increase your mercy in us, that in difficult moments we might not despair nor become despondent, but with great confidence submit ourselves to your holy will, which is Love and Mercy itself.

- Optional Closing for Children of Divorce:

  I forgive my parents. Jesus, I trust in you.

St. Faustina's vision of God's divine mercy poured forth for the world.

SESSION VII

"Lead Us Not into Temptation, but Deliver Us from Evil"

Be not far from me, for trouble is near
and there is none to help.
Psalm 22:11

PRAYER

Opening

L: Lord, open my lips.

R: And my mouth will proclaim your praise.

L: Gracious God, you call us to acknowledge Jesus as our Savior and Redeemer. May our hearts be filled with joy as we praise you and look forward to the fullness of your kingdom. We pray this through Christ our Lord. Amen.

Psalm 19

L: In Psalm 19, the psalmist, praises the glory of God in his creation and in his Law. He begs God for help to keep from transgression so that sin will not have dominion over him.

L: The heavens are telling the glory of God; and the firmament proclaims his handiwork.

R: Day to day pours forth speech, and night to night declares knowledge.

L: There is no speech, nor are there words; their voice is not heard;

R: Yet their voice goes out through all the earth, and their words to the end of the world.

L: In them he has set a tent for the sun, which comes forth like a bridegroom leaving his chamber, and like a strong man runs its course with joy.

R: Its rising is from the end of the heavens, and its circuit to the end of them; and there is nothing hidden from its heat.

L: The law of the Lord is perfect, reviving the soul;
the testimony of the Lord is sure, making wise the simple;

R: The precepts of the Lord are right, rejoicing the heart;
the commandment of the Lord is pure, enlightening the eyes;

L: The fear of the Lord is clean, enduring for ever;
the ordinances of the Lord are true, and righteous altogether.

R: More to be desired are they than gold, even much fine gold;
sweeter also than honey and drippings of the honeycomb.

L: Moreover by them is your servant warned; in keeping them there is great reward. But who can discern his errors? Clear me from hidden faults.

R: Keep back your servant also from presumptuous sins; let them not have dominion over me! Then I shall be blameless, and innocent of great transgression.

All: Let the words of my mouth and the meditation of my heart be acceptable in your sight, O Lord, my rock and my redeemer.

Prayer of Intercession

L: For that which tempts me toward hopelessness:

R: Lord, have mercy.

L: For those I have abandoned or who have abandoned me:

R: Lord, have mercy.

L: For the times in which I have doubted God's love:

R: Lord, have mercy.

L: For my weakness of faith:

R: Lord, have mercy

Closing Prayer

L: All of our prayers are made perfect and complete in the prayer that Jesus taught us. Let us pray together:

All: Our Father who art in heaven. . . .

L: Glory be to the Father and to the Son and to the Holy Spirit.

R: As it was in the beginning, is now and ever shall be, world without end. Amen.

REFLECTION

In our last session, we focused on the power of forgiveness to heal the wound of divorce and restore our hopes for the future. Forgiving our parents, however, will not likely shut the door on the past that has so deeply marked us. On the contrary, if we are to embrace the deepest truth about ourselves, we will have to be ever vigilant against the temptation to become cynical. We will have to implore the very One whom we may be tempted to doubt: "lead us not into temptation, but deliver us from evil." Having rediscovered our identity as children of our Heavenly Father, we plead, in this final petition of the Lord's Prayer, for the grace to recognize and live in this truth always.

At the Core of Temptation

The *Catechism of the Catholic Church* speaks of temptation within the context of setting one's heart on a treasure (see *CCC*, 2848).

> For where your treasure is, there will your heart be also. . . .
> No one can serve two masters.
>
> —*Matthew 6:21, 24*

Temptation has a lot to do with *what* we set our hearts on—what we desire. There are, of course, good and bad treasures, good and bad desires corresponding to the "two masters." But there is also the question of *how* to go about getting the good "treasure" we have set our hearts on. We may have our hearts directed toward something very good, but we can go about getting it rightly or wrongly. Will we wait for it to be given to us, or take matters into our own hands, preemptively? Much of temptation happens here. Indeed, the first temptation was a matter of precisely this. It was not that the "apple" was bad; it just could not be *taken*. It had to be *given*.

Doubting the Goodness of God

The attempt to grasp at the "treasure" is especially true when it comes to the deepest desire of the human heart: the desire for happiness. The content of that desire is the encounter with a great Love, the Love of the One who made us. But Love can only be given and given in time. The reason we are tempted to take it, however, is the fear that we will be denied our heart's desire, our "treasure." We have a subtle, and sometimes not-so-subtle, doubt about the goodness of God's Fatherhood. It was this doubt that the Devil tried to insinuate when he tempted Jesus—unsuccessfully—to take things into his own hands. And it is the same doubt that he uses against us now—with more success. We stop waiting for God to give and begin to take things into our own hands so that we take what we can get.

Coming from a broken home adds fuel to the already smoldering fire of temptation. We have discussed in previous sessions how our

Michelangelo Caravaggio, *The Incredulity of Saint Thomas* (c. 1601–1602), The Sanssouci, Postsdam, Germany

parents' divorce has distanced us from our own origins, effectively burdening us with distorted images of spousal love, fatherhood, and motherhood. For many of us, these images have gathered strength and hardened over the years, insinuating themselves into our various relationships. These false images lie at the heart our temptations. They offer themselves as the definitive word on love. In doing so, they call into question the very goodness of God's Fatherhood.

If we give into this fundamentally mistaken judgment about reality—about ourselves, others, and God himself—we are prone to give in to cynicism. With cynicism, we "already know how things really are." We start convincing ourselves: *I am not worthy of love*; *I belong to no one*; *I am an orphan*; *the world holds no promise for me*. As for our own loves, we start telling ourselves: *Love does not last*. And when difficulties come, we give up. Essentially, we doubt the goodness of God. We decide not to "wait" for the Father, for his Word, for his Bread, for his Fatherly Love. Instead, we take things into our own hands and fend for ourselves to take what we can get.

False Securities

One of the ways we take things into our own hands is by placing our hope in false securities. Because of the divorce of our parents, many of us feel as though we are adrift and, consequently, look for anything to grab onto as an anchor for our lives. Some of these "anchors" include: perfectionism, workaholism, excessive desire for control, exaggerated need to please people, lust (pornography, promiscuity, premarital and extramarital sex, immodesty, etc.), greed, overeating, endless distraction (overuse of TV, internet, smartphones, etc.), and addiction (gambling, drugs, alcohol, etc.). These, however, only give us a temporary illusion of security, as they invariably start to pull us down. It is as though we were building our "house" on shifting sand.

> Every one then who hears these words of mine and does them will be like a wise man who built his house upon the rock; and the rain fell, and the floods came, and the winds blew and beat upon that house, but it did not fall, because it had been founded on the rock. And every one who hears these words of mine and does not do them will be like a foolish man who built his house upon sand; and the rain fell, and the floods came, and the winds blew and beat against that house, and it fell; and great was the fall of it.
>
> —*Matthew 7:24–27*

A "house" built on sand collapses. As children of divorce, we know what it means for a house to collapse. The only thing that can truly anchor us is the very thing of which our parents were the (imperfect) sign. How much more, then, do we want *the* "Rock," the deepest foundation of our lives, the deepest Origin of our security. How much more do we need the certainty that we are the beloved sons and daughters of God!

"Lead Us Not into Temptation"

Ultimately, in order to resist these fundamental temptations, we must live according to the truth of our being. We must, that is, constantly return to the true image of Love, to the truth of God's Fatherhood revealed to us in Christ the Son. He, in his flesh, *is* the Image of the Father's Love. We need only recognize him and draw near to him. In this way, we will recover a true view of the world and of our own situation. And knowing *the definitive Word on Love*, we will be able to find lasting security and take the risk of love in marriage—then motherhood and fatherhood—without being scandalized and defeated by all the limitations we will surely find therein.

What temptations have I given in to as the result of my parents' divorce? Have I been tempted by false securities or given in to them in my own life?

LEARNING TO SEE: THE SACRAMENT OF PENANCE

For we all make many mistakes.

—*James 3:2*

In the last session, we spoke of our drawing close to the One who is "rich in mercy" (*Ephesians* 2:4) so that we might begin to forgive. Recall that the Our Father draws a connection between the forgiveness of others and our own need for forgiveness: "Forgive us our trespasses, *as we forgive* those who trespass against us." In these two final petitions—"Lead us not . . ." and "deliver us . . ."—we address this need directly. Like everyone else, we need this guidance and deliverance. But as children of divorced parents, we especially need deliverance from cynicism and resentment. We too, then, are in need of mercy. The venue for this mercy is the very simple, humble, and beautiful Sacrament of Penance or Reconciliation—"Confession." When we go to Christ with our sins, declaring them to the priest, we open ourselves to the beauty of God's mercy for us. It is there that we rediscover the mercy of the One who is rich in mercy. "I absolve you, in the name of the Father and of the Son and of the Holy Spirit."

> Jesus said to them again, "Peace be with you. As the Father has sent me, even so I send you." And when he had said this, he breathed on them, and said to them, "Receive the Holy Spirit. If you forgive the sins of any, they are forgiven."
>
> —*John 20:21–23*

This session's practice is to go to Confession and let the Father extend his forgiveness to us through his Son, and his priests, by the power of the Holy Spirit. To help prepare for the Sacrament, we offer an examination of conscience intended specifically for adult children of divorce. It is followed by a general examination of conscience.

Specific Examination of Conscience for Adult Children of Divorce[1]

- Have I rejected or doubted God's goodness and love for me?
- Have I rejected or doubted the truth that I am God's beloved and wonderfully made?
- Have I sought affirmation in the wrong ways and/or separate from God's affirmation of me?
- Have I sought security in anything other than God? Have I placed my security in any of the following: being a perfectionist, "control freak," workaholic, or "people pleaser," lust or inducing lust through immodesty, greed, overeating, excessive distractions such as TV, internet, sports, or addictions such as gambling, drugs, alcohol?
- Have I given in to despair?

1. This examination was written by Daniel Meola, co-founder and president of Life-Giving Wounds.

- Have I given in to cynicism toward relationships, marriage, or having children?
- Have I settled for anything less than God's plan for love and marriage as total self-gift? Have I had premarital sex or sexual relations of any sort outside of marriage, settled for temporary relationships in the form of cohabitation? Have I masturbated, used pornography, or lusted in any other way? Have I resented chastity?
- Have I shut myself off to others by choosing to be self-protective when my personal safety is not threatened to the detriment of self-giving?
- Have I avoided conflict, wounds, and problems when I needed to confront them for my health and others' well-being?
- Have I harbored feelings of anger to the point of rage, hatred, or resentment toward my parents or another person?
- Have I spoken disrespectful words toward or about my parents or another?
- Have I given into bitterness toward my parents or another? Have I been vengeful? Have I intentionally hurt another?
- Have I refused to forgive my parents or another person?
- Have I refused to ask for forgiveness when I have been at fault?
- Have I blamed my sins on someone else so that I would not have to take responsibility for them?
- Have I refused to practice unconditional love in any other way?

General Examination of Conscience (from The Knights of Columbus' *Guide to Confession*, 1999)[2]

1. *I am the Lord your God. You shall not have strange gods before me.*
    - Do I seek to love God with all my heart and with all my soul and with all my strength? (See *Deuteronomy*

2. This booklet was written for and published by the Knights of Columbus Catholic Information Service. It is reproduced with the express written permission of the publisher.

6:5.) Do I put anything or anyone above God? Do I pray daily?

- Have I had any involvement with the occult, witchcraft, wicca, ouija boards, séances, tarot cards, new age crystals, fortune telling, or the like? Have I put faith in horoscopes?
- Have I received Holy Communion in a state of mortal sin?
- Have I abused the Sacrament of Penance by lying to the priest or deliberately not confessing a mortal sin?
- Have I denied a truth of the faith out of concern for the respect or opinion of others?

2. *You shall not take the name of the Lord your God in vain.*
    - Have I used God's holy name irreverently?
    - Have I blasphemed God, the Church, Mary, the saints, or sacred places or things?
3. *Remember to keep holy the Lord's Day.*
    - Do I try to keep Sunday as a day of prayer, rest, and relaxation, avoiding unnecessary work?
    - Have I deliberately come late or left early from Mass without a good reason?
4. *Honor your father and your mother.*
    - Do I honor and respect my parents?
    - Have I deliberately hurt my parents?
    - Do I treat my children with love and respect?
    - Do I support and care for the well-being of all family members?
    - Have I neglected family duties?
    - Do I honor and obey my lawful superiors?

5. *You shall not kill.*

- Have I deliberately harmed anyone?
- Have I had an abortion or encouraged an abortion?
- Have I attempted suicide or seriously considered it?
- Have I abused drugs or alcohol?
- Have I led anyone to sin through bad example or through direct encouragement?

6. *You shall not commit adultery.*

For the married

- Am I faithful to my spouse in thoughts and action?
- Have I used artificial contraception, or been sterilized?
- Was I married outside the Church without proper permission of the Church?

For the unmarried

- Have I engaged in sexual activity with anyone of either sex?

For all

- Have I deliberately viewed pornographic magazines, videos or internet websites?
- Have I masturbated?
- Have I used impure language or told impure jokes?
- Do I dress modestly?

7. *You shall not steal.*

- Have I stolen or accepted stolen goods?
- Have I deliberately destroyed the property of others?
- Have I cheated anyone of what I owe?
- Do I gamble excessively?

- Do I share what I have with the poor and the Church according to my means?
- Have I pirated materials: videos, music, software?

8. *You shall not bear false witness against your neighbor.*
   - Have I lied? Have I sworn falsely?
   - Have I plagiarized or been academically dishonest?
   - Have I gossiped? Have I revealed secrets or confidential information without good reason?
   - Have I ruined the good name of others by spreading lies or maliciously revealing their faults and sins?
9. *You shall not desire your neighbor's wife.*
   - Have I deliberately and consciously permitted sexual thoughts about anyone besides my spouse?
   - Do I guard my imagination and senses?
   - Have I watched shows, plays, pictures or movies that contain impure scenes with the deliberate intention of being aroused by them? Am I responsible about what I read?
10. *You shall not desire your neighbor's goods.*
    - Am I envious of the possession, abilities, talents, beauty, or success of others?

You shall love your neighbor as yourself.

- Do I love my neighbor? Is there anyone whom I do not love or refuse to love? Have I wished harm or misfortune on anyone?
- Do I forgive from my heart those who have hurt me? Do I harbor hatred or grudges? Do I pray for my enemies?
- Have I ridiculed or humiliated others?

- Do I seek to help others in need?
- Do I love myself as God loves me? Do I care for my physical, emotional, and spiritual health?
- Do I forgive myself for my sins after bringing them to God in the Sacrament of Reconciliation?

Precepts of the Church

- Have I deliberately missed Mass on a Sunday or Holy Day of obligation without a serious reason?
- Do I go to confession at least once a year or when I have serious sins to confess?
- Do I receive Holy Communion at least once during Eastertime?
- Do I take part in the major feasts celebrating Our Lord, the Virgin Mary, and the saints?
- Do I abstain from meat on Fridays during Lent (for ages 14 and over) and fast on one full meal on Ash Wednesday and Good Friday (for ages 18–59)? Do I fast for one hour before Holy Communion (water and medicine allowed)?
- Do I contribute to support the material needs of the Church?

SESSION VIII

Who Am I? Plumbing the Depths and Beginning Again

O LORD, you have searched me and known me!
Psalm 139:1

PRAYER

Opening

L: Lord, open my lips.

R: And my mouth will proclaim your praise.

Psalm 139

L: In Psalm 139, the psalmist tells us that before we knew ourselves, God knew us. In that knowledge we can be certain that there is something more to know about ourselves than what we "already know."

L: O Lord, you have searched me and known me!
You know when I sit down and when I rise up; you discern my thoughts from afar.
You search out my path and my lying down, and are acquainted with all my ways.

R: *Even before a word is on my tongue, behold, O Lord, you know it altogether.*
You beset me behind and before, and lay your hand upon me.
Such knowledge is too wonderful for me; it is high, I cannot attain it.

L: Where shall I go from your Spirit? Or where shall I flee from your presence?
If I ascend to heaven, you are there! If I make my bed in Sheol, you are there!
If I take the wings of the morning and dwell in the uttermost parts of the sea,

R: *even there your hand shall lead me, and your right hand shall hold me.*
If I say, "Let only darkness cover me, and the light about me be night,"
even the darkness is not dark to you, the night is bright as the day;
For darkness is as light with you.

L: For you formed my inward parts, you knitted me together in my mother's womb.
I praise you, for I am wondrously made. Wonderful are your works!
You know me right well; my frame was not hidden from you, when I was being made in secret, Intricately wrought in the depths of the earth.

R: *Your eyes beheld my unformed substance;*
in your book were written, every one of them, the days that were formed for me,
when as yet there was none of them.
How precious to me are your thoughts, O God! How vast is the sum of them!
If I would count them, they are more than the sand. When I awake, I am still with you.

L: Search me, O God, and know my heart! Try me and know my thoughts!

R: *And see if there be any wicked way in me, and lead me in the way everlasting.*

L: Glory be to the Father and to the Son and to the Holy Spirit.

R: *As it was in the beginning, is now and ever shall be, world without end. Amen.*

Reading

Reader:
A Reading from Ephesians (1:3–13)

Paul, an apostle of Christ Jesus by the will of God, To the saints who are also faithful in Christ Jesus: Grace to you and peace from God our Father and the Lord Jesus Christ.

Blessed be the God and Father of our Lord Jesus Christ, who has blessed us in Christ with every spiritual blessing in the heavenly places, even as he chose us in him before the foundation of the world, that we should be holy and blameless before him. He destined us in love to be his sons through Jesus Christ, according to the purpose of his will, to the praise of his glorious grace which he freely bestowed on us in the Beloved. In him we have redemption through his blood, the forgiveness of our trespasses, according to the riches of his grace which he lavished upon us. For he has made known to us in all wisdom and insight the mystery of his will, according to his purpose which he set forth in Christ as a plan for the fulness of time, to unite all things in him, things in heaven and things on earth.

In him, according to the purpose of him who accomplishes all things according to the counsel of his will, we who first hoped in Christ have been destined and appointed to live for the praise of his glory. In him you also, who have heard the word of truth, the gospel of your salvation, and have believed in him, were sealed with the promised Holy Spirit, who is the guarantee of our inheritance until we acquire possession of it, to the praise of his glory.

A Litany

L: Lord, have mercy.

R: Lord, have mercy.

L: Christ, have mercy.

R: Christ, have mercy.

L: Lord, have mercy.

R: Lord, have mercy.

L: Christ, hear us.

R: Christ, graciously hear us.

L: When I feel the ground opening from under me:

R: Our Father who art in heaven.

L: When I feel abandoned, left alone:

R: Hallowed be thy name.

L: When I am unable to entrust myself to you, God:

R: Thy kingdom come. Thy will be done.

L: When I am hungry for love:

R: Give us this day our daily bread.

L: When I am unwilling to forgive:

R: Forgive us our trespasses, as we forgive those who trespass against us.

L: When I doubt the goodness of God:

R: Lead us not into temptation.

L: For the promise of eternal love:

R: Our Father who art in heaven.

L: For hope that all things can be made new:

R: Our Father who art in heaven.

L: In thanksgiving for being wonderfully made:

R: Hallowed be thy name.

REFLECTION

We have now come to a conclusion, having completed our journey through the Our Father. This prayer has, of course, been given to all Christians. But for us, it resonates in a particularly dramatic way. Our experience of divorce has wounded us at the point of our origin. And it has therefore raised in us some of the most basic questions about ourselves, the goodness of our lives, and the possibility of love. We are tempted to look away from it, to forget. But now, because of the Our Father—and the reality it acknowledges—we can plumb the depths of that wound to find there the deepest truth of ourselves. So without forgetting—without denying anything—we can begin again. We do this for ourselves. But we do it also for the world. Our need for clarity about who we are—and the One on whom our lives ultimately depend—is not only our need. It is also the world's need. Thus, surprisingly, what may be for us the most painful part of our history, can become a resource for the whole world.

Our Cultural Situation

Until very recently, there was a basic cultural awareness that, at a minimum, it was good for a man and a woman to stay together for the children. Staying together was essential for children's stability, their way of being "at home" in the world. This was the mentality until about fifty years ago when the basic "minimum" started to become negotiable. The reason for this was that the very *meaning of marriage* had changed. The bond of marriage had become a mere consensus of two wills. What reason, then, could there be to constrain those two wills by that bond, if they were now up against "irreconcilable differences"? Why shouldn't they be free now to unmake the bond and go their separate ways? Adult children of divorce can already sense that there is something wrong with this superficial view of things, since the unmaking of their parents' union has almost "unmade" *them*. They have been torn asunder.

"Who Am I?"

More than anything now, it is the existential angst of the children of divorce that has us looking at the union that brought them into existence. If the children of this newly easy-to-dissolve marriage are not "ok," then perhaps marriage is not just whatever the spouses want it to be. Perhaps it is not just about "two wills," making (and unmaking) their union. Perhaps it is, rather, something greater, something they are ushered into. After all, the love that leads a man and a woman to marriage is something they "fall into" when they are struck by something greater than themselves. If this is the case, what is it that a man and woman are ushered into? Many, inside and outside of Christianity have noted the glimpse of the Eternal hovering behind every true love: when lovers say, "I love you," they include, however tacitly, "forever." Indeed, for the Christian, marriage has been caught up in God, as a sacrament of his *eternal* love for us, through Jesus Christ.

Perhaps no modern thinker has taken up the question of the relationship between marriage and human identity with more depth than Pope St. John Paul II. St. John Paul II's great contribution was to ground the revelation of God's love to the child continually and consistently in marriage and the family. In the family, he said, the child encounters the Love at the source of everything, the most fundamental affirmation. Beginning with the love of the mother and the father for each other, the child discovers the Love that wants him or her "just because." The child encounters this affirming Love before he can walk or talk, before he can reason. Indeed, he encounters this Love even in the womb.

> From the very moment of conception, and then of birth, the new being is meant to express fully his humanity, to "find himself" as a person. To be human is his fundamental vocation: to be human in accordance with the gift received, in accordance with that talent which is humanity itself, and only then in accordance with other talents. In this sense God wills every man "for his own sake" . . . in conjugal love and in paternal and maternal love we should find inscribed the same truth about man which the council expressed in a clear and concise way in its statement that God "willed man for his own sake."
>
> —St. John Paul II
> *Letter to Families*, 9

God, in his mysterious providence, has so willed it that two fallible people would manifest his eternal and perfect love to the human being from the very beginning of his or her existence.

> As we read in the Book of the prophet Jeremiah: "Before I formed you in the womb I knew you, and before you were born I consecrated you" (*Jeremiah* 1:5). The genealogy of the person is thus united with the eternity of God and only then with human fatherhood and motherhood, which are realized in time. At the moment of conception itself, man is already destined to eternity in God.
>
> —St. John Paul II
> *Letter to Families,* 9

Then, he willed that parents manifest that love in their life together throughout the course of a child's upbringing (and beyond).

> Through marriage, children learn without words that God is faithful, patient, respectful and generous love. Faith in the God who is Love is handed on first of all by the witness of a fidelity to spousal love, which translates naturally into love for the children who are the fruit of the union.
>
> —Pope Benedict XVI
> *General Audience,* June 8, 2011

The depth of marriage is the reason that children in the wake divorce rightly ask: "Who am I now, now that may parents have denied the unity that made me?" The question is raised almost immediately.

> When I came home from college, I noticed that my mother had taken hardly anything from my home except for the things that were most precious and valuable—the china, the silver, the trunk. Then there was that feeling that the ground had opened at my feet and a vast chasm had opened up. I felt as though I was about to fall into that chasm and disappear from the face of the earth.
>
> —Lisa Lickona

There is a reason, though, why the end of our parents' divorce is not really the end—why the chasm does not swallow us up. It is the same reason, paradoxically, that our parents' unity is so important and their disunity, so devastating.

> In the end, even though one's parents are charged with radiating God's eternal and perfect love, they are *not* that eternal and perfect love. And in the face of the abyss, there is Another who will respond. "Abyss calls upon abyss," as the psalmist says.
>
> —Lisa Lickona

What is left for the child of divorce, then, are two ultimate possibilities. One is to forget by keeping one's memories in check with diversion and distraction. The other is to face the "abyss" —the wound one has—and then with the help of others, discover that at the depth of that abyss is the Love that makes us (in creation) and remakes us (in Baptism). If we are to find our way out of the darkness and discover our place in the world, we must return to that Love, the Love of the Father revealed in his Son through the Holy Spirit.

"Father!" Many children of divorce speak this name in fear and trembling. And yet it will only be in speaking this name that we will discover the One whose love precedes and surpasses our parents' love. He is the One from whom all fatherhood on earth and heaven are named (see *Ephesians* 3:14–15). He is the one who chose us in Christ before the foundations of the world (see *Ephesians* 1:4). He is the one who chooses us and wants us even if our own father and mother have forgotten us. This is what the Christian faith has to offer us: the link to our deepest Origin, to what ultimately defines us.

> *Father*—with this word I express my certainty that someone is there who hears me, who never leaves me alone, who is always present. I express my certainty that God, despite the infinite difference between him and me, is such that I can speak to him, may even address him familiarly as "thou" (the German *du*). His greatness does not overwhelm me, does not reject me as insignificant and unimportant. Certainly I am subject

to him as a child is subject to his father, yet there is such a fundamental similarity and likeness between him and me, yes, I am so important to him, I belong so closely to him, that I can rightly address him as "Father." My being born is not a mistake, then, but a grace. It is good to live even though I do not always perceive it.

I am wanted; not a child of chance or necessity, but of choice and freedom. Therefore, I shall also have a purpose in life; there will always be a meaning for me, a task designed just for me, there is a conception of me that I can seek and find and fulfill.

When the school of life becomes unbearably hard, when I would like to cry out as Job did, as the psalmist did—then I can transform this cry into the word "Father" and the cry will become gradually a word, a reminder to trust, because from the Father's perspective it is clear that my distress, yes, my agony, is part of the greater love for which I give thanks.

—Ratzinger
Co-Workers of the Truth, 103

From within the experience of faith, do I perceive my wound as a resource for myself and for others? Do I experience, at the depth of the "abyss," Another who responds? If not, am I open to it?

Saying "Our Father" for the World

As children of divorced parents, we live with a wound that is sometimes unbearable. The wound has put some very basic things into question: the goodness of our lives, the possibility of love, even the possibility of God's love. Now by "learning to see" the Love that is more definitive, we can begin to look at our wound in new terms. Just as our death—the wound of wounds—became the "point of entry" where God gave us his life through his Son, so too the wound of divorce—the wound of a broken origin—can be a point of entry where God's Fatherhood can be more clearly seen and known.

When Christ, the Son of the Father, accepted death on the Cross, he entered the distance between God and man, brought about by the "no" that our first parents spoke at the dawn of time. And doing so with his "yes"—"not my will, but thine"—he made that death, and every suffering great or small, a "place" which actually *goes somewhere*. Now these "deaths" are a place to *find him*, and with him the Origin our first parents once refused. Indeed, we can say, without being superficial, that the wound of divorce is for us a place which compels us to see more clearly what others who, standing on firmer ground, take for granted if they are not altogether blind to it. We see the One on whom our life ultimately depends, and who has now mercifully caught us up in his Son and recreated us as his sons and daughters. What is more, our wound can even be a place of mission, a resource for the world. Let us then, throughout our lives, pray the Our Father for ourselves and for the world.

Our Father who art in heaven,
Hallowed be thy name.
Thy kingdom come.
Thy will be done on earth, as it is in heaven.
Give us this day our daily bread,
And forgive us our trespasses,
As we forgive those who trespass against us,
And lead us not into temptation,
But deliver us from evil.

LEARNING TO SEE: THE *ANGELUS*

As we pray the Our Father for the world, we are called to respond to the love of the Father by saying "yes"—the "yes" first uttered by Mary, our Mother. The practice for this last session then is to pray the *Angelus* every morning. The *Angelus* is the prayer that recalls the moment of the Incarnation when Mary said *fiat*—"be it done unto me according to thy word" (see *Luke* 1:38). Making the *Angelus* the very first thing we do, say, and think will help us remember our true identity. If we pray it truly, by making Mary's words *our words*, God's presence will make things new *in us*. He who was born to recreate us as sons and daughters of his Father, will redeem what is broken in us and make us flourish.

Mary's "yes" at the moment of the Annunciation endured to the last, when the sword pierced her heart as Simeon had foretold (see *Luke* 2:33–35). Her unconditional love in the face of great suffering is the path for us. It is the way to face the conditional love that has caused us so much suffering.

> May she, the Handmaid of the Lord, be an example of humble and generous acceptance of the will of God. May she, the Sorrowful Mother at the foot of the Cross, comfort the sufferings and dry the tears of those in distress because of the difficulties of their families.
>
> —St. John Paul II
> *Familiaris Consortio*, 86

"Be it done unto me according to thy word." As we pronounce the words of our Mother Mary, let us learn how to say "yes" to Our Father.

Lastly, as we go forth from this program, let us remember by praying this prayer, that Christ gave Mary to us as our Mother. What Christ said to John at the foot of the Cross, he says to all of us: "Behold, your mother" (*John* 19:27). Mary accompanied her Son as he suffered his wounds on Calvary; she now accompanies us as we bear ours.

The *Angelus*

L: The Angel of the Lord declared unto Mary.

R: And she conceived of the Holy Spirit.

L: Hail Mary, full of grace, the Lord is with thee.
Blessed art thou among women and blessed is the fruit of thy womb, Jesus.

R: Holy Mary, Mother of God, pray for us sinners, now and at the hour of our death. Amen.

L: Behold the handmaid of the Lord.

R: Be it done unto me according to thy word.

L: Hail Mary. . . .

R: Holy Mary. . . .

L: And the Word was made Flesh.

R: And dwelt among us.

L: Hail Mary. . . .

R: Holy Mary. . . .

L: Pray for us, O holy Mother of God.

R: That we may be made worthy of the promises of Christ.

L: Let us pray:

All: Pour forth, we beseech thee, O Lord, thy grace into our hearts; that we, to whom the Incarnation of Christ, thy Son, was made known by the message of an angel, may by his Passion and Cross be brought to the glory of his Resurrection. Through the same Christ our Lord.

Amen.

◀ Jean-François Millet, *The Angelus* (1857–59), Musée d'Orsay, Paris, France

SUPPLEMENT 1

Children of Marriages Declared Null and Other Broken Familial Situations

We recognize that children come from a variety of broken familial situations other than divorce and, therefore, we have written this supplement in order to explain why *The Recovering Origins* initiative can help all these other adult children to heal from their suffering too.

One situation that deserves special attention, from a Catholic point of view, is the case of a marriage declared null (popularly referred to as an "annulment"). Many people think that obtaining a declaration of nullity from the Catholic Church is the same as a civil divorce, except with religious approval. The large volume of marriage cases handled by diocesan tribunals along with the admittedly high percentage of affirmative decisions (i.e., where the marriage is in fact declared null) gives this impression. In addition, an investigation of nullity often appears to intrude unnecessarily into the personal lives of others. These factors taken together project the image of a process that is perfunctory, arbitrary, and intrusive.

This, however, is not the case. An investigation of nullity operates on an entirely different set of principles and assumptions than the process for a civil divorce. Whereas the notion of a civil divorce is built upon the state's claimed ability to break a union entered into by two individuals, the Church recognizes that the marriage bond never truly existed when the marriage is declared null by a Church tribunal. Hence, the language employed by the Church reflects this difference—she *declares* an objective truth and does not claim to "tear asunder what God has joined." In this way, the goal of every investigation of nullity is, in fact, to uphold the truth of marriage.

God designed marriage when he created man and woman for one another as a "unity of the two" (see *Genesis* 2; and John Paul II, *Mulieris Dignitatem*, 6), and ordered it to its completion in the Sacrament of Marriage instituted by Christ (see *Matthew* 19; *Ephesians* 5; and John Paul II, *Mulieris Dignitatem*, 7). Marriage is therefore a reality that has a particular, objective sacramental structure in which a man and a woman's love is assumed into divine love by virtue of their participation in Christ through Baptism and their vows of fidelity, indissolubility, and openness to children.

Because the Church recognizes that marriage must be freely embraced and consented to in order for a couple to enter it, an investigation of nullity seeks to unearth the nature of the spouses' consent at the time it was exchanged. Adequate consent is necessary for a marriage to be valid. This means that the man and woman must understand and accept the essential dimensions of marriage (without, necessarily, having a full grasp of them nor a perfectly mature ability to embrace them). These essential dimensions, contained and expressed in the vows of marriage, are (1) fidelity (2) openness to children and the obligation to educate them, and (3) indissolubility.[1] Then too there must be a *capacity*, to consent, including the freedom to do so.[2] If it can be shown that one or both of the spouses either did not consent adequately to the marriage by failing to accept any one of its essential dimensions, or was incapable of consent, then the marriage can be judged never to have existed and is declared null. Otherwise, the

1 See *Code of Canon Law*, canons 1055, § 1; 1096; 1101, § 2.

2 Grounds that invalidate consent based on the *incapacity* to posit consent are: the lack of the sufficient use of reason, grave defect of discretion or judgement concerning the essential rights and obligations of marriage, and the inability to assume the essential obligations of marriage due to causes of a psychological nature. (See *Code of Canon Law*, 1095). We note that there are also other grounds that invalidate consent (various forms of error, conditions, or fraud, force, fear etc.).

marriage is considered to exist and, if it is a marriage between the baptized, is a sacrament from which the spouses can draw the divine grace necessary to carry out conjugal life anew.

In light of its purpose and horizon, we know the annulment process *can* be a great comfort to children who yearn to know and live the authentic truth of marriage. The investigation of nullity helps to make clear both what happened to one's own parents and what marriage is. At the same time, however, we recognize that children from marriages declared null *still suffer like children of divorce.* They may suffer for one of two reasons.

The first is the real possibility of an error made on the part of the tribunal. This happens. And it is, of course, a great scandal. For this sad case, the Church does have a place of redress in the Tribunal of the Sacra Rota in Rome. It is perfectly proper for a child who suspects that the "annulment" given to his or her parents was unjustified, to urge them (or one of them) to make an appeal to the Roman Rota. Such an appeal can be healing and serve to further demonstrate the Church's commitment to marriage.

Apart from the question of legitimacy of a given annulment, children of parents whose marriages are declared null legitimately suffer as a result of their parents' *lack of unity*, since in the case of a proper annulment, what is confirmed is precisely the lack of unity from the very beginning. From the child's perspective, the effect is similar, objectively speaking, to that of a child conceived outside of wedlock, even if his or her parents were rightly concerned with being married at the time. It is the suffering from the *lack* of the proper unity in his parent's love.

Even though theirs is an objectively different situation from those children whose parents divorced civilly or never married, however, it should be noted that children whose parents receive a declaration of nullity experience a similar sense of abandonment, especially if the putative marriage was, in fact, stable for many years. Since it is the lived experience of intactness that anchors children in their temporal origin, giving them the certainty that reality is good and trustworthy, the discovery that this was not the case from the beginning undermines their identity. In a word, the experience of belonging to a mother and father who belong to each other and to their family, inserts children into their place in the world. This sense pervades their entire existence, including their affect and memory, such that a declaration of nullity, even when objectively true, speaks against everything they know, love, and have come to cherish through experience.

Children of divorce suffer from the *broken* unity of their parents' marriage, while children of annulment suffer from the *lack of* unity, since their parents did not have a true marriage. In the latter case there is a *lack* of the proper marital unity that ought to have shaped the child's life vis-a-vis his parents. And this lack of unity affects the child's identity since he or she is the fruit of his parents' bodily unity. The child begins to wonder: *If my parents' communion is lacking, then am I, the fruit of that communion, lacking too? Am I not worth the struggle, sacrifice, and commitment proper to the unity of a marriage?* The child may even go one step further and doubt God's goodness. *If God is good, why didn't he give me united parents like other children have?* From the child's point of view, whether he or she is from a broken unity (as in the case of divorce) or a lacking one (annulments and other similar situations), what is most necessary is to recover his or her Origin in God, whose loving unity with us always endures. Central to this recovery is for these adult children to put their sufferings at the service of this deeper and truer judgment.

SUPPLEMENT 2

Group Formats

There are many possible formats for working through *Recovering Origins* as a group. A group may gather once a week, once every other week, once a month, or over a weekend for a retreat. Below are some instructions to keep in mind in every case. They are followed by a sample retreat schedule and ideas for a longer program.

In anticipation of any group program, the leaders might form a prayer group to pray for the participants by name. Adult children of divorce often feel as if they do not have a home. In view of that, persons in the community in which the program/retreat is taking place (for example, the parish) might think of ways to reach out to the participants ahead of time. One idea is to write letters of welcome and encouragement to the participants to tell them that someone has been praying for them. Another is to host an informal dinner for them.

The program should open with the guide giving witness to the healing, either in his or her own life or in the lives of others. The participants might also be encouraged to share something of their lives, *if they wish*, as they introduce themselves to each other. There should be great delicacy here not to force immediate intimacy before it unfolds freely and naturally.

Between sessions, there should be ample opportunity for the prayer suggested in the "Learning to See" sections, and for keeping a journal.

WEEKEND RETREAT

For a weekend retreat, we recommend having a priest in attendance in order to make Adoration, Confession, and Mass available. An additional spiritual director could also be on hand, depending on the number of participants. One possible retreat schedule is as follows:

Friday

6:30 – 7:00 P.M.	Meet and Greet; overview of the weekend
7:00 – 8:30 P.M.	Discussion and First Meditation: Where Do We Stand as Children of Divorce?
8:30 P.M.	Depart or free time

Saturday

8:30 – 9:00 A.M.	Breakfast
9:00 – 10:00 A.M.	Second Meditation: "Our Father Who Art in Heaven"
10:00 – 10:30 A.M.	Personal prayer and reflection
10:30 – 11:30 A.M.	Third Meditation: "Hallowed Be Thy Name"
11:30 – 12:00 P.M.	Daily Mass (with special intentions for healing) or personal prayer
12:00 – 1:00 P.M.	Silent lunch • Personal prayer and reflection • Meetings with the priest and/or spiritual director
1:00 – 2:00 P.M.	Fourth Meditation: "Thy Kingdom Come, Thy Will Be Done on Earth as It Is in Heaven"
2:00 – 2:30 P.M.	Guided Scriptural Meditation: The Wedding Feast of Cana

2:45 – 3:30 P.M.	Fifth Meditation: "Give Us This Day Our Daily Bread"
3:30 – 4:00 P.M.	Personal prayer and reflection
4:00 – 5:00 P.M.	Sixth Meditation: ". . . As We Forgive Those Who Trespass Against Us"
5:00 – 5:15 P.M.	Divine Mercy Chaplet followed by an Examination of Conscience
5:15 – 6:30 P.M.	Dinner: conversation • Personal prayer and reflection • Meetings with the priest and/or spiritual director
6:30 – 8:00 P.M.	Praise and worship, Adoration and sacramental Confession
8:00 P.M.	Depart or free time

Sunday

9:30 – 10:00 A.M.	Breakfast
10:00 – 11:00 A.M.	Seventh Meditation: "Lead Us Not into Temptation"
11:00 – 12:00 P.M.	Personal prayer and reflection • Meetings with the priest and/or spiritual director
12:00 – 1:00 P.M.	Lunch discussion about the weekend
1:00 – 2:00 P.M.	Discussion and Eighth Meditation: Who am I?
2:00 – 3:00 P.M.	Sunday Mass
3:00 – 3:30 P.M.	Last remarks and final prayer

A LONGER PROGRAM

When a retreat is not possible or preferred, groups can meet over a more extended period of time. This has many advantages. It helps participants to work through things in more detail and depth. It allows more time for prayer and reflection between sessions. And participants can develop valuable friendships with each other. In this case we recommend that Adoration be offered after Session III, Mass be offered after Session V, and sacramental Confession be made available after Session VII.

General Resources

THE FATHERHOOD OF GOD

Balthasar, Hans Urs von. *Unless You Become Like this Child*. San Francisco: Ignatius Press, 1991.

Benedict XVI. "The Lord's Prayer." In *Jesus of Nazareth: From the Baptism in the Jordan to the Transfiguration*, 128–68. New York: Doubleday, 2007.

Catechism of the Catholic Church: Revised in Accordance with the Official Latin Text Promulgated by Pope John Paul II. Washington, DC: United States Catholic Conference, 1997. See especially paragraphs 2759–2865.

Clément, Olivier. *Three Prayers: Our Father, O Heavenly King, The Prayer of Saint Ephrem*. Translated by Michael Breck. Crestwood, NY: St. Vladimir's Seminary Press, 2000.

Gavin, John, SJ. *The Mystery of the Lord's Prayer, Wisdom from the Early Church*. Washington, DC: The Catholic University of America Press, 2021.

Giussani, Luigi. *Dal Temperamento un Metodo*. Milan: Rizzoli, 2002.

———. *La Convenienza Umana della fede*. Milan: Rizzoli, 2018.

Groeschel, Benedict. *Stumbling Blocks or Stepping Stones: Spiritual Answers to Psychological Questions*. Mahwah, NJ: Paulist Press, 1987.

Hahn, Scott. *A Father Who Keeps His Promises: God's Covenant Love in Scripture*. Cincinnati, OH: Servant Books, 1998.

John Paul II. *Dives in Misericordia*. Encyclical Letter (November 30, 1980).

———. *Crossing the Threshold of Hope*. Edited by Vittorio Messori. New York: Knopf, 1994.

St. Teresa of Avila. *The Way of Perfection*. Translated by E. Allison Peers. New York: Image Books, 1964.

Tertullian, Cyprian, and Origen. *On the Lord's Prayer*. Translated by Alistair Stewart-Sykes. Crestwood, NY: St. Vladimir's Seminary Press, 2004.

Wojtyła, Karol. *Radiation of Fatherhood*. In *The Collected Plays and Writings on Theater*, 333–364. Translated by Boleslaw Taborski. Berkeley: University of California Press, 1987.

———. *The Jeweler's Shop*. Translated by Boleslaw Taborski. San Francisco: Ignatius Press, 1992.

———. *The Poetry of John Paul II: Roman Triptych, Meditations*. Translated by Jerzy Peterkiewicz. Washington, DC: USCCB Publishing, 2003.

DIVORCE

Bloom, Allan. *The Closing of the American Mind*. New York: Simon and Schuster, 1987.

Coleman, Melissa. *This Life Is in Your Hands: One Dream, Sixty Acres, and a Family Undone*. New York: Harper, 2011.

Marquardt, Elizabeth. *Between Two Worlds: The Inner Lives of Children of Divorce*. New York: Three Rivers Press, 2005.

McCarthy, Margaret Harper. *Torn Asunder: Children, the Myth of the Good Divorce and the Recovery of Origins.* Grand Rapids, MI: William B. Eerdmans Publishing Co., 2017.

Miller, Leila. *Primal Loss. The Now-Adult Children of Divorce Speak.* Phoenix, AZ: LCB Publishing, 2017.

Root, Andrew. *The Children of Divorce: The Loss of Family as the Loss of Being.* Grand Rapids, MI: Baker Academic, 2010.

Rowdon, Nicky. "Cold War." *Humanum* I (Spring 2012): 9–11. https://humanumreview.com/articles/cold-war.

Staal, Stephanie. *The Love They Lost: Living with the Legacy of Our Parents' Divorce.* New York: Dell Publishing, A Delta Book, 2000.

Thomas, Susan Gregory. *In Spite of Everything: A Memoir.* New York: Random House, 2011.

Wallerstein, Judith S., Julia M. Lewis, and Sandra Blakeslee. *The Unexpected Legacy of Divorce: A 25 Year Landmark Study.* New York: Hyperion, 2000.

Whitehead, Barbara Dafoe. *The Divorce Culture: Rethinking Our Commitments to Marriage and Family.* New York: Knopf, 1997.

SUFFERING—HEALING—FORGIVENESS

Baars, Conrad W. *Feeling and Healing Your Emotions.* Gainesville, FL: Bridge-Logos, 2003.

Baars, Conrad W., and William Dichil. *Born Only Once: The Miracle of Affirmation.* Chicago: Franciscan Herald Press, 2001.

Cavins, Jeff, and Matthew Pinto. *Amazing Grace for Those Who Suffer.* West Chester, PA: Ascension Press, 2002.

D'Elbée, Jean C. J. *I Believe in Love: A Personal Retreat Based on the Teaching of St. Thérèse of Lisieux*. Translated by Marilyn Teichert and Madeleine Stebbins. 2nd ed. Manchester, NH: Sophia Institute Press, 2001.

Groeschel, Benedict J. *Arise from Darkness: What to Do When Life Doesn't Make Sense*. San Francisco: Ignatius Press, 1995.

John Paul II. *Salvifici doloris*, Apostolic Letter on the Christian Meaning of Human Suffering, February 11, 1984.

Thérèse of Lisieux. *The Story of a Soul*. Translated by John Clarke. 3rd ed. Washington, DC: ICS Publications, 1996.

Trent, John, with Larry K. Weeden. *Breaking the Cycle of Divorce: How Your Marriage Can Succeed Even If Your Parents' Didn't*. Carol Stream, IL: Tyndale House, 2006.

OTHER

St. Basil. *On the Holy Spirit*. Crestwood, NY: St. Vladimir's Seminary Press, 1980.

Guardini, Romano. *Sacred Signs*. Translated by Grace Branham. St. Louis, MO: Pio Press, 1956.

Ouellet, Marc. *Divine Likeness: Toward a Trinitarian Anthropology of the Family*. Translated by Philip Milligan and Linda M. Cicone. Grand Rapids, MI: William B. Eerdmans, 2006.

Ratzinger, Joseph. *The Spirit of the Liturgy*. Translated by John Saward. San Francisco: Ignatius Press, 2000.

———. *Co-Workers of the Truth*. Translated by Mary Frances McCarthy and Lothar Krauth. San Francisco: Ignatius Press, 1992.

Index